Leckie × Leckie
Scotland's leading educational publishers

CW01651074

Practice Papers for SQA Exams

Standard Grade General Credit

Geography

01/240610

ISBN 978-1-84372-770-5

Published by
Leckie & Leckie
An imprint of HarperCollins*Publishers*
Westerhill Road, Bishopbriggs, Glasgow, G64 2QT
T: 0870 460 7662 F: 0870 787 1720
enquiries@leckieandleckie.co.uk www.leckieandleckie.co.uk

A CIP Catalogue record for this book is available from the British Library.

Questions and answers in this book do not emanate from SQA. All of our entirely new and original Practice Papers have been written by experienced authors working directly for the publisher.

Leckie & Leckie would like to thank Chris Upson for his kind permission to reproduce the Irn-Bru factory photograph on page 38 (www.geograph.org.uk)

Introduction

Layout of the book

This book contains practice exam papers, which mirror the actual SQA exam as much as possible. The layout, paper colour and question level are similar to the actual exam that you will sit, so that you are familiar with what the exam paper will look like.

The answer section is at the back of the book. The answers include practical tips on how to tackle certain types of questions, details of how marks are awarded and advice on what the examiners will be looking for.

Revision advice is provided in this introductory section of the book, so please read on!

How To Use This Book

The practice papers can be used in two main ways:

1. You can complete an entire practice paper as preparation for the final exam. If you would like to use the book in this way, you can either complete the practice paper under exam style conditions by setting yourself a time for each paper and answering it as well as possible without using any references or notes. Alternatively, you can answer the practice paper questions as a revision exercise, using your notes to produce a model answer. Your teacher may mark these for you.
2. You can use the Topic Index to find all the questions within the book that deal with a specific topic. This allows you to focus specifically on areas that you particularly want to revise or, if you are mid-way through your course, it lets you practise answering exam-style questions for just those topics that you have studied.

The Exam

Syllabus

Listed below is an outline of the topics assessed in the Standard Grade Geography exams. The Credit and General course cover the same topics but, at Credit level, the topic is covered in more depth and the exam questions are more demanding.

You can obtain a detailed syllabus from the SQA website at www.sqa.org.uk or ask your teacher for a copy.

Physical Geography

Map skills
Weather
Climate Regions
Rivers
Glaciation

Human Geography

Map Skills
Settlement
Industry
Farming

International Issues

Population
Environmental issues
Trade
Aid
International Influences and Alliances

Time

The time allocations are different for the Foundation, General and Credit exams.

Level	Time
Foundation	1 hour 5 min
General	1 hour 25 min
Credit	2 hours

Be aware of the time as you proceed through the exam.

For example, if you are half way through a Credit exam after 20 minutes, then you are almost certainly not giving enough full and detailed answers. On the other hand, you do not want to get into a position where you are rushing to finish the last few questions and give messy and incomplete answers towards the end of the paper. Take care to pace yourself sensibly and avoid both of these two extremes.

Every year some candidates leave the exam early. This can never be a good thing to do in an exam like Geography where an answer can always be improved or the grid references for your map work questions checked over for silly mistakes. Look out for the pupils in your own school who regularly leave exams early. They will almost certainly be pupils who do not perform well in exams. It must be stressed again that if you have finished and checked your answers well before the end of the exam, then you are either not giving enough detail or paying attention to neatness and presentation.

Front Cover

The front cover of the exam paper asks you to fill in information.

Do this as neatly as possible and set off in the right direction. Remember this is the first thing that the marker will see when he/she sits down to mark your paper, so make a good impression.

Also on the front cover are some instructions about the exam. This is given for a good reason and you should pay attention to what it says here. The instructions are similar for the General and Credit exam papers.

The General exam requires the answers to be written on spaces provided on the question paper. However, the Credit exam requires the answers to be written on a separate answer booklet.

These are some of the instructions that you will see on the front page of your exam paper:

Read each question carefully.
Answer all questions.
Write as neatly as possible.
Answer in sentences wherever possible.

Grades

The Standard Grade Geography exams assess two components: knowledge and understanding (KU) and enquiry skills (ES).

The KU component is testing your ability to recall information about the content of the course material.

The ES component is testing your ability to apply your knowledge to a new situation, sometimes in a difficult and challenging way. You also have to specify gathering and processing techniques that you would use when undertaking fieldwork in a given situation.

For each exam, the KU component is worth 40% of the total marks and the ES component is worth 60% of the total marks available.

You are given a grade for each component based on the table below:

Level	Percentage	Grade
Credit	70…100	1
Credit	50…69	2
General	70…100	3
General	50...69	4
Foundation	70…100	5
Foundation	50…69	6

The cut-off scores for each grade can vary depending upon the level of difficulty of the exam; so do not feel that you must score at least 70% in the Credit exam to be awarded a grade 1.

Each year the examiner's report on the SQA website specifies the cut-off scores for each grade in the Foundation, General and Credit exams.

Overall Grade Calculation

Your overall grade for Standard Grade Geography is solely derived from your performance in the exam

Your overall grade for the course is derived from the following formula:

$$\text{Overall grade} = (\text{KU grade} \times 4 + \text{ES grade} \times 6) \div 10$$

The examples given below show how the overall grade has been calculated. (The overall grade is always rounded to the nearest whole number).

George	**Grade**
Knowledge and Understanding	1
Enquiry Skills	2
	$(1 \times 4 + 2 \times 6) / 10 = 1.6$
Overall Grade	**2**

Jennifer	**Grade**
Knowledge and Understanding	4
Enquiry Skills	2
	$(4 \times 4 + 2 \times 6) / 10 = 2.8$
Overall Grade	**3**

Topic Index

Topic	Sub-topic	Exam A		Exam B		Knowledge for Prelim			Knowledge for SQA Exam		
		General	Credit	General	Credit	Have difficulty	Still needs work	OK	Have difficulty	Still needs work	OK
1. Mapwork	Cross-section			1a							
	Matching features on an OS map	1a									
	Land use on an OS map	1e	1b, 1c	1d, 1e	1c, 1d						
	Land use conflict		1d								
2. Glaciation	Glaciation features on an OS map		1a (i)								
	Upland glaciation features	2	1a (ii)								
	Lowland glaciation features			2							
3. Rivers	Rivers and their valleys on an OS map				1a						
	River feature formation	1f		1b	1b						
4. Settlement	Functions of a settlement	1d			1d						
	Identifying the CBD on an OS map			1f							
	Residential areas on an OS map	1b	4								
	The sphere of influence				4						

Topic	Sub-topic	Exam A		Exam B		Knowledge for Prelim			Knowledge for SQA Exam		
		General	Credit	General	Credit	Have difficulty	Still needs work	OK	Have difficulty	Still needs work	OK
5. Climatic Regions	Climate graphs	4b		4a, 4b							
	Recent changes in regions	5		5b							
6. Environmental Issues			3		3						
7. The Weather	Choosing a weather station site			3a							
	Air masses			3b							
	BBC weather map	3									
	Synoptic charts		2a, 2b		2						
8. Industry	Industrial location an OS map	1c									
	Industrial location factors		6		5						
	Industrial decline	6a									
9. Farming	Farm types			6	6a						
	Recent changes in farming	7	5								

Topic	Sub-topic	Exam A		Exam B		Knowledge for Prelim			Knowledge for SQA Exam		
		General	Credit	General	Credit	Have difficulty	Still needs work	OK	Have difficulty	Still needs work	OK
10. Population	Gathering population information			8							
	Population distribution		7								
	Population pyramids	9a			7a, 7b						
	Demographic transition model		8a								
	Effects of population change	9b	8b								
	Migration	8									
11. Trade	World trade		9a	9a	8						
	Single product economies			9b							
	Multinational corporations				9						
12. Aid	Short or long term aid?	11									
	Suitable aid										
	Intermediate technology			10							
	Why give aid?				10						
Enquiry skills – Gathering Information		6b	1e	1c	1f						
Enquiry skills – Processing Information		4a, 10	9b	5a, 7	6b						

General Level Exam A

Geography

Standard Grade: General Level

Practice Papers
For SQA Exams

General Level
Exam A

Fill in these boxes:

Name of centre	Town
Forename(s)	**Surname**

You are allowed 1 hour, 25 minutes to complete this paper.

Make sure you read the questions carefully.

Try to answer all of the questions in the time allowed.

Write your answers in the spaces provided.

Make sure you write as neatly as you can and answer in sentences wherever possible.

Where required insert a tick ✓ in the box ☐ beside the correct answer.

Leckie × Leckie
Scotland's leading educational publishers

1:50 000 Scale
Landranger Series

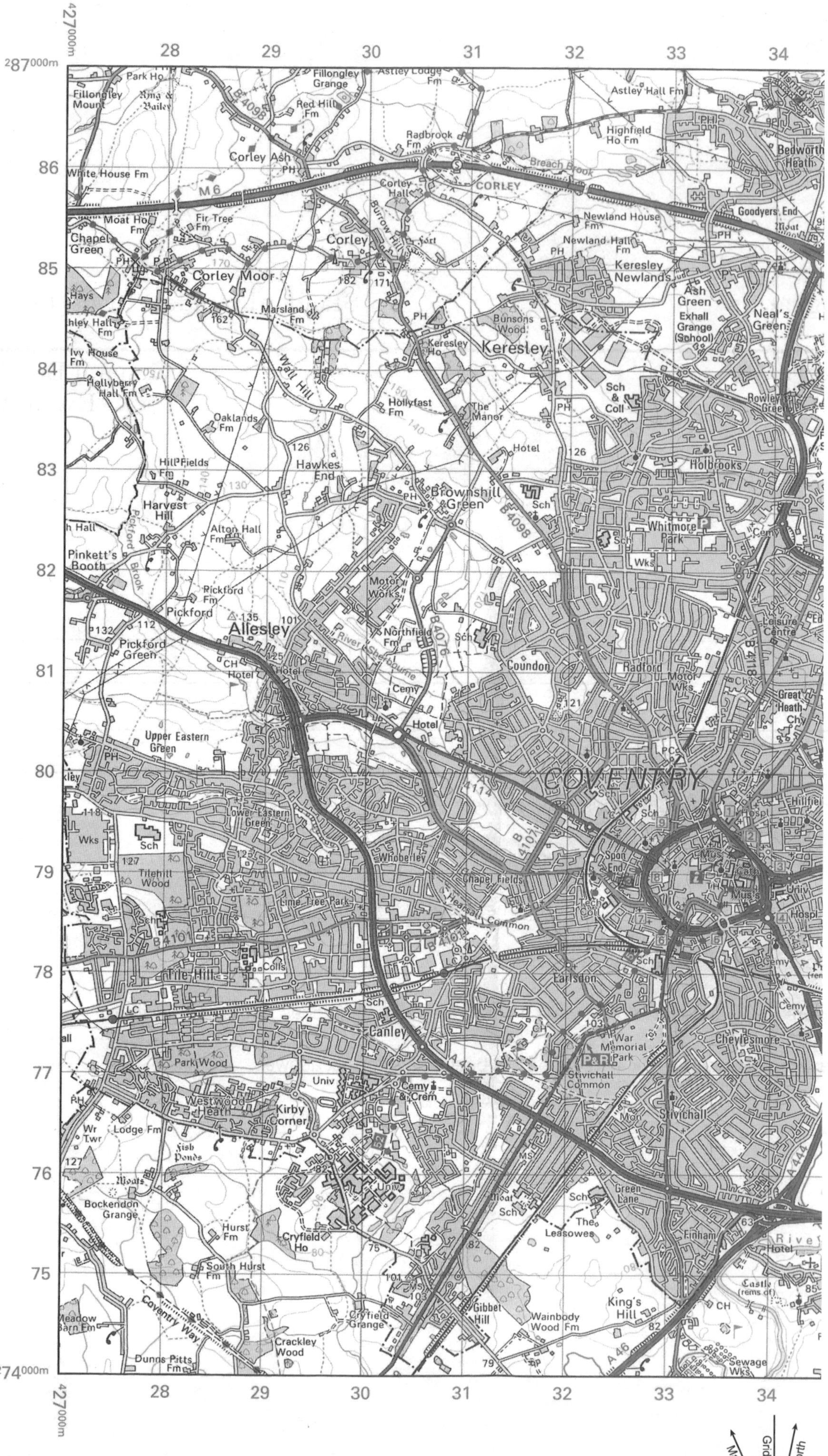

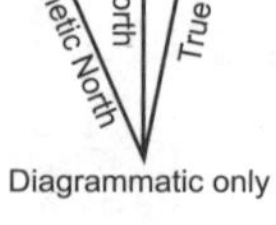

Diagrammatic only

Four colours should appear above; if not then please return to the invigilator.

Four colours should appear above; if not then please return to the invigilator.

Extract No 1742/140

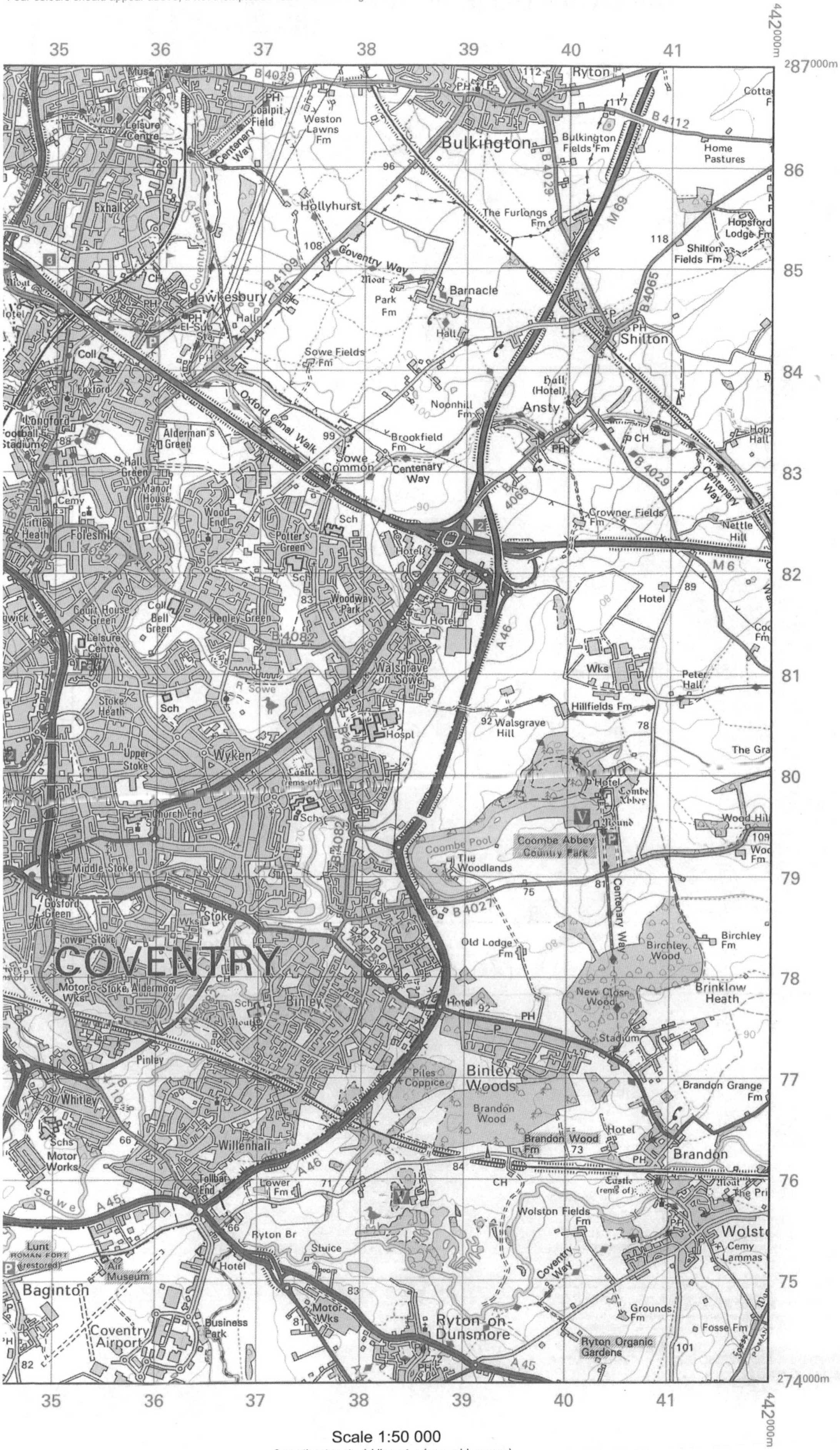

Scale 1:50 000

2 centimetres to 1 kilometre (one grid square)

2 1 0 Kilometres 1 2 3

1 0 Miles 1 2

1 kilometre = 0.6214 mile

1 mile = 1.6093 kilometres

Reference Diagram Q1A

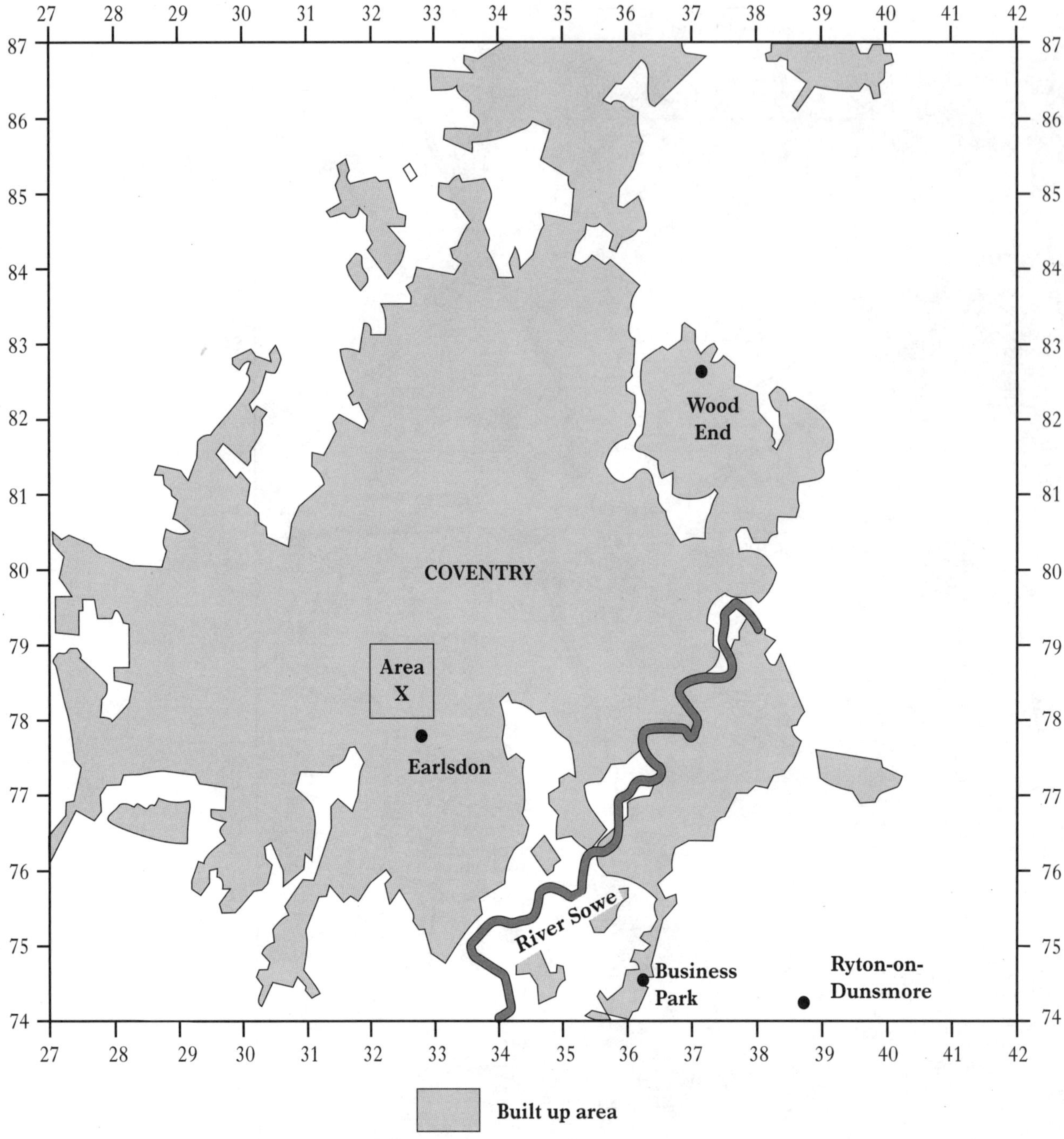

DO NOT WRITE IN THIS MARGIN

This question refers to the OS map extract of Coventry and Reference Diagram Q1A.

Marks | KU | ES

1. (*a*) Complete the table below by matching the physical features to the correct grid references.

Choose from the following grid squares.

3775 3784 3575 3975

Physical Feature	Grid Square
Broad floodplain	
Gently sloping land	
Meander	
Tributaries meeting river	

3

(*b*) Two residential areas of Coventry are found in grid squares 3277 (Earlsdon) and 3682 (Wood End).

Using map evidence, **describe** the differences between these areas.

____

____

____

____

____

______________________________ 4

(*c*) There is a Business Park in grid square 3674.

Explain why this site is suitable for a Business Park.

You **must** use map evidence.

____

____

____

____

____

______________________________ 4

DO NOT WRITE IN THIS MARGIN

1. (continued)

Marks | KU | ES

(*d*) 'The main function of Ryton-on-Dunsmore in grid square 3874 is to serve as a commuter settlement for Coventry.'

Do you agree with this statement?

Tick (✓) your choice. Yes ☐ No ☐

Give reasons for your choice.

____

____

____

____

____

______________________________ 4

(*e*) It is proposed to develop Area X into a Country Park (See Reference Diagram Q1A).

Using map evidence, give arguments **for** and **against** this proposal.

____

____

____

____

____

______________________________ 4

(*f*) **Explain** how the meander was formed in grid square 3778.

You may use diagram(s) to illustrate your answer.

____

____

____

____

____

______________________________ 3

DO NOT WRITE IN THIS MARGIN

Marks | KU | ES

2. Reference Diagram Q2: A glaciated upland area.

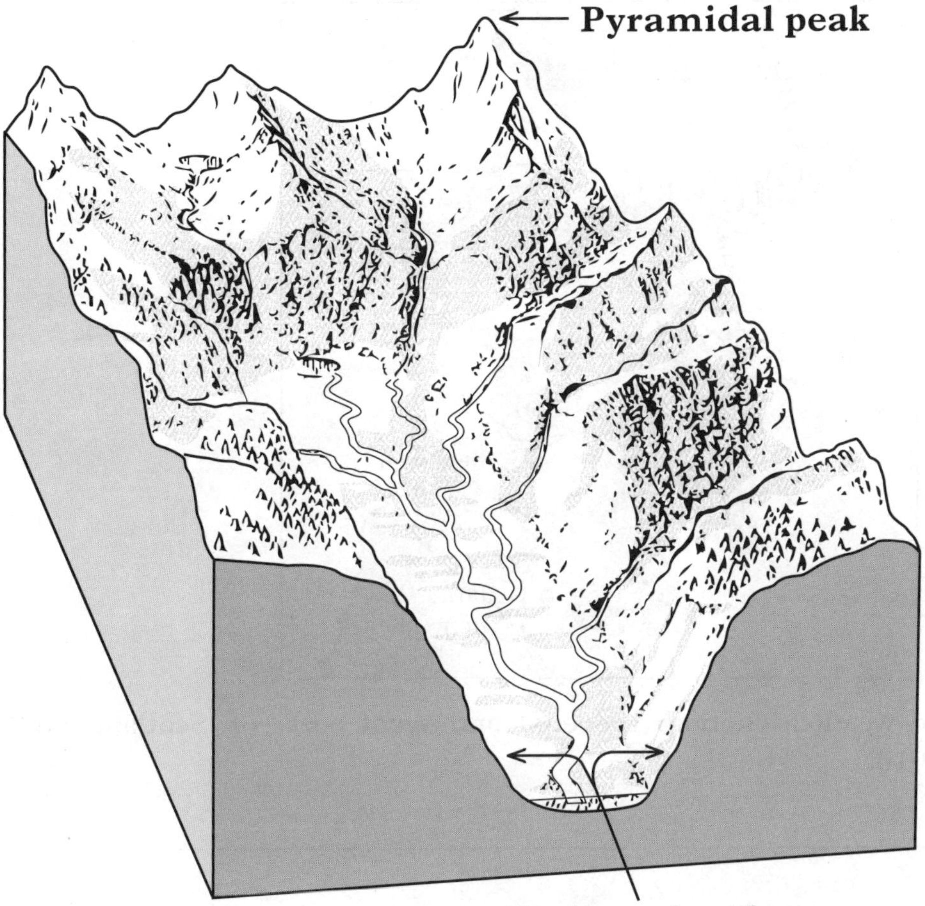

Explain how either a u-shaped valley or a pyramidal peak is formed.

You may use diagram(s) to illustrate your answer.

____

____

____

____

____

____

____

____ 4

DO NOT WRITE IN THIS MARGIN

Marks | KU | ES

3. Reference Diagram Q3A: Weather map of Scotland 3rd March 2010.

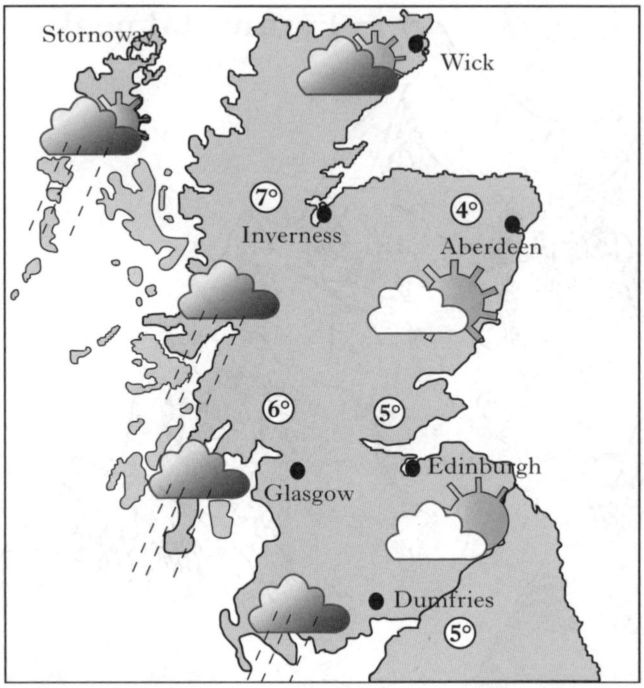

Compare the weather on both the **east** and **west** coast of Scotland on 3rd March 2010.

____

____

____

____

____

____ **4**

DO NOT WRITE IN THIS MARGIN

Marks | KU | ES

4. Reference Diagram Q4A: Climate data for Cairo.

Month	J	F	M	A	M	J	J	A	S	O	N	D
Rainfall (mm)	15	12	10	10	0	0	0	0	0	0	12	15
Temperature (°C)	13	14	17	21	25	28	29	29	27	23	20	13

Reference Diagram Q4B: Climate graph for Cairo.

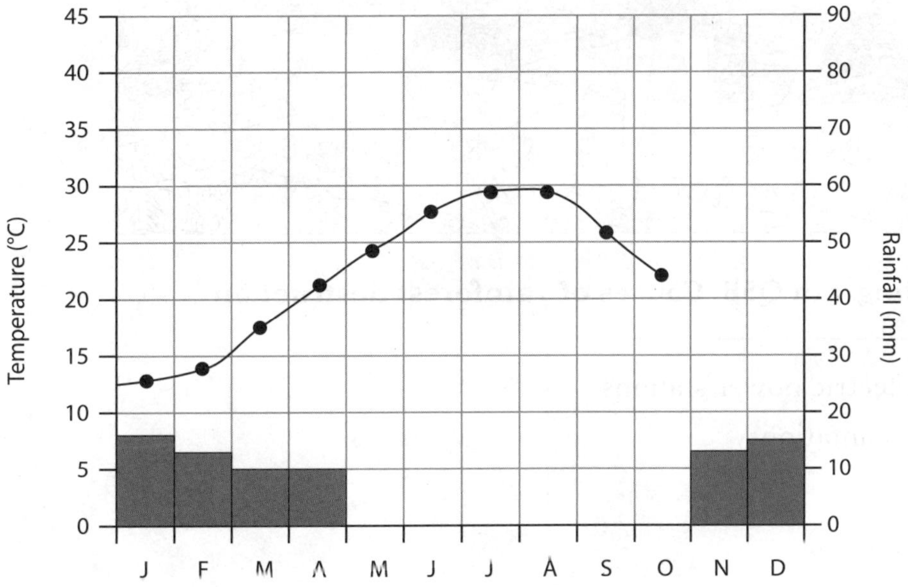

(*a*) Look at the table above (Reference Diagram Q4A).

Use this data to complete the climate graph for Cairo.

(*b*) Describe **in detail** the climate shown in Reference Diagram Q4B. 2

____

____

____

____

____

____ 4

DO NOT WRITE IN THIS MARGIN

5. Reference Diagram Q5A: Rainforest landscape after deforestation.

Marks | KU | ES

Reference Diagram Q5B: Causes of rainforest destruction

- Hydro-electric power stations
- Rubber plantations
- Mines
- Cattle ranching
- Logging
- New roads

'Rainforest developments have brought many benefits to the local people.'

Do you fully agree with this statement?

Give reasons for your answer.

____

____

____

____

____

______________________________ **4**

DO NOT WRITE IN THIS MARGIN

Marks | KU | ES

6. **Reference Diagram Q6: An old industrial landscape**

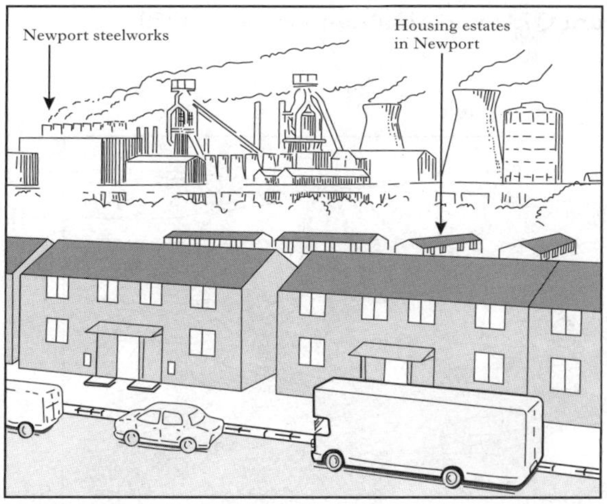

(*a*) **Explain** the social, economic and environmental effects of a factory closing down.

____

____

____

____

____

____ 4

(*b*) Identify **two** gathering techniques that pupils could use to investigate the effects of a factory closing on local people **and** businesses.

Give reasons for your answer.

Technique 1 ____________________

Reason(s) ____

____

____

Technique 2 ____________________

Reason(s) ____

____

____ 4

DO NOT WRITE IN THIS MARGIN

7. Reference Diagrams Q7A and Q7B.

Marks | KU | ES

Reference Diagram Q7A: Farming Landscape in 1950

Small fields

Few big machines

Low output per hectare

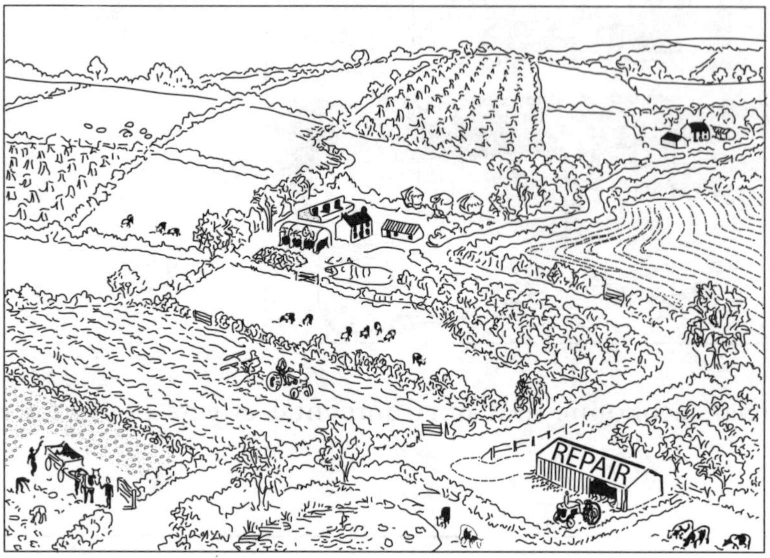

Many workers

Small farms

Reference Diagram Q7B: Farming Landscape in 2010

Large fields

Many large machines

High output per hectare

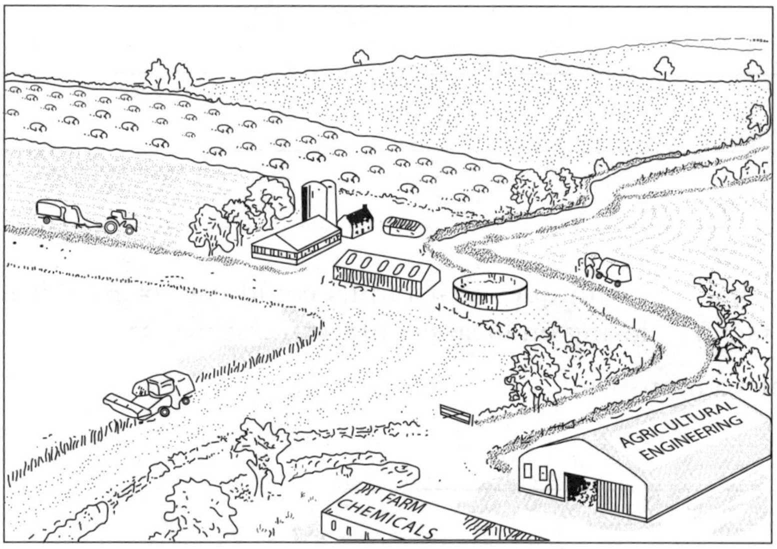

Few workers

Large farms

What are the advantages **and** disadvantages of the changes that have taken place in farming in the past 50 years?

4

DO NOT WRITE IN THIS MARGIN

8. Reference Diagram Q8: Migration within a developing country.

Marks | KU | ES

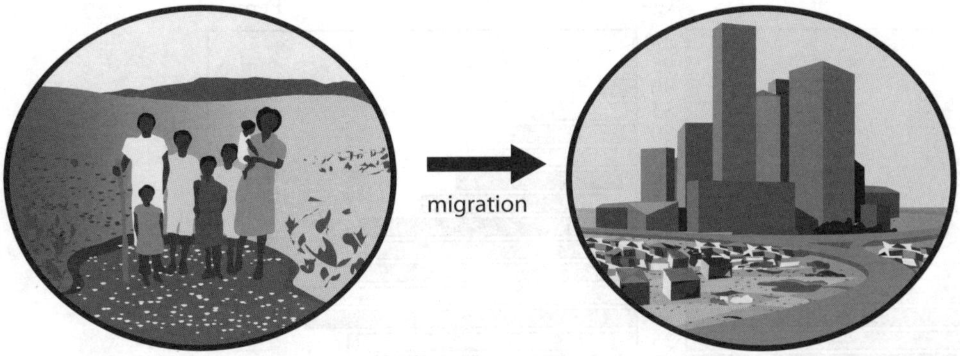

People living in rural areas in developing countries such as Pakistan can face many problems that can encourage them to migrate to a city such as Karachi.

Do you think people benefit by moving?

Give reasons for your answer.

____

____

____

____

____

____ **4**

DO NOT WRITE IN THIS MARGIN

Marks | KU | ES

9. Reference Diagram Q9: Population Pyramid of the UK.

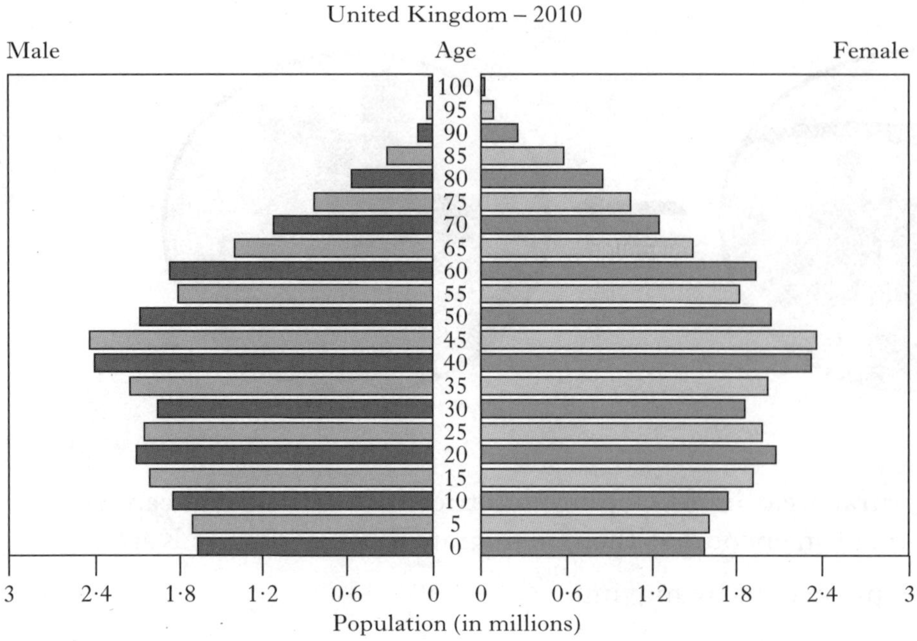

Study Reference Diagram Q9 above

(*a*) Describe **in detail** the population structure of a developed country, like the UK.

3

(*b*) What **problems** will this population structure create in the future?

4

DO NOT WRITE IN THIS MARGIN

10. Reference Diagram Q10A: Kenya's imports.

Marks | KU | ES

Consumer goods	15%
Industrial supplies	33%
Fuels	24%
Machinery and transport equipment	28%

Reference Diagram Q10B: Kenya's exports.

Coffee and tea	21%
Flowers	14%
Manufactured goods	13%
Other	52%

Study Reference Diagrams Q10A and Q10B.

Give two **other** processing techniques which could be used to display the information in the tables above.

Give reasons for your choice of techniques.

Technique 1 ________________________

Reason(s) ________________________

____

____

Technique 2 ________________________

Reason(s) ________________________

____

________________________ **4**

DO NOT WRITE IN THIS MARGIN

11. Reference Diagram Q11A: January 2010: Effects of Haitian earthquake.

Marks | KU | ES

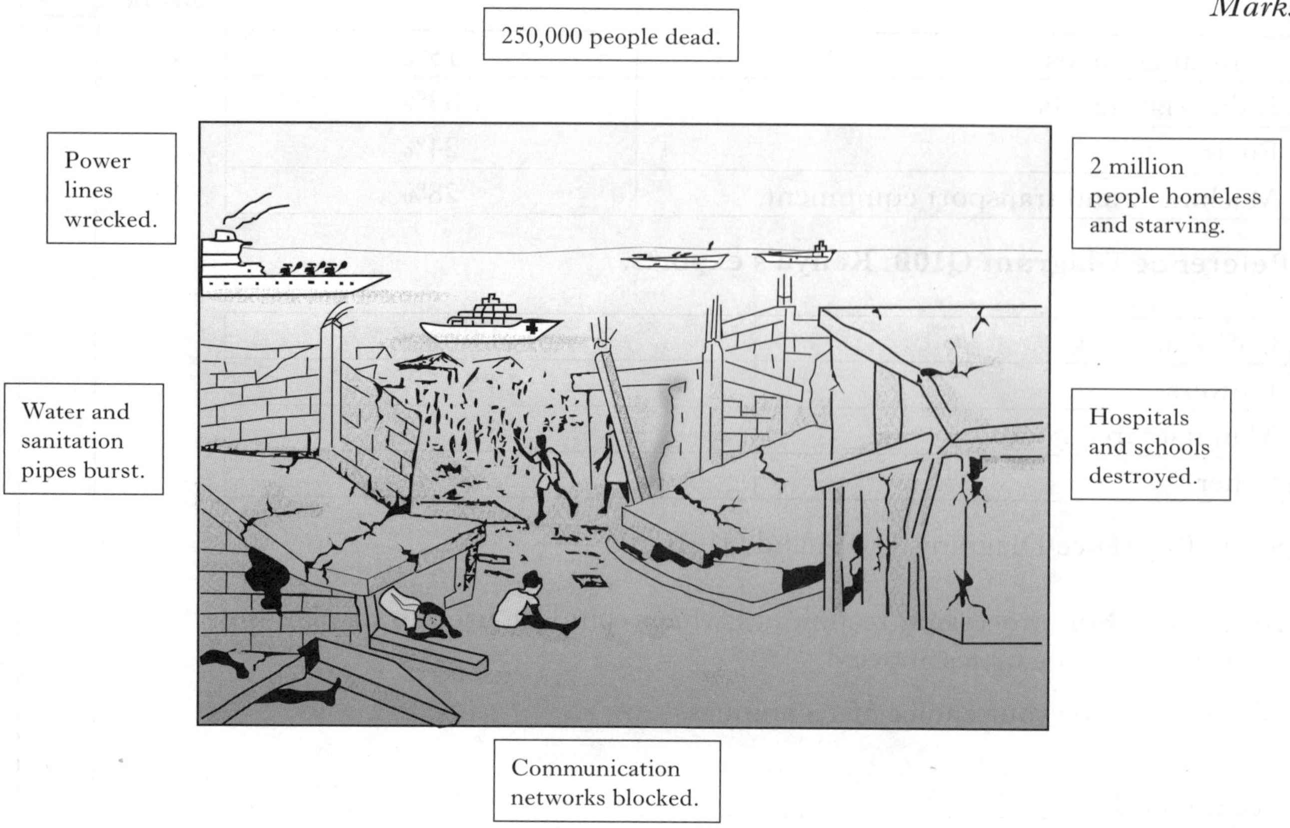

Reference Diagram Q11B: Types of aid

Short-Term Aid	**Long-Term Aid**
Food	Farm equipment and fertilisers
Clean water	Build new houses, roads and bridges
Tents and blankets	Build hospitals and schools
Medicines	Reconnect electricity supplies

Study Reference Diagrams Q11A and Q11B.

Which type of aid would be more suitable for countries like Haiti after an earthquake?

Short-term aid ☐ Long-term aid ☐

Tick (✓) your choice.

Give reasons for your choice.

____

____

____

____

____ **3**

Credit Level Exam A

Geography

Standard Grade: Credit Level

Practice Papers
For SQA Exams

Credit Level
Exam A

You are allowed 2 hours to complete this paper.

Marks will be allocated for appropriate sketches and diagrams.

Make sure you write as neatly as you can and answer in sentences wherever possible.

Leckie×Leckie
Scotland's leading educational publishers

1:50 000 Scale
Landranger Series

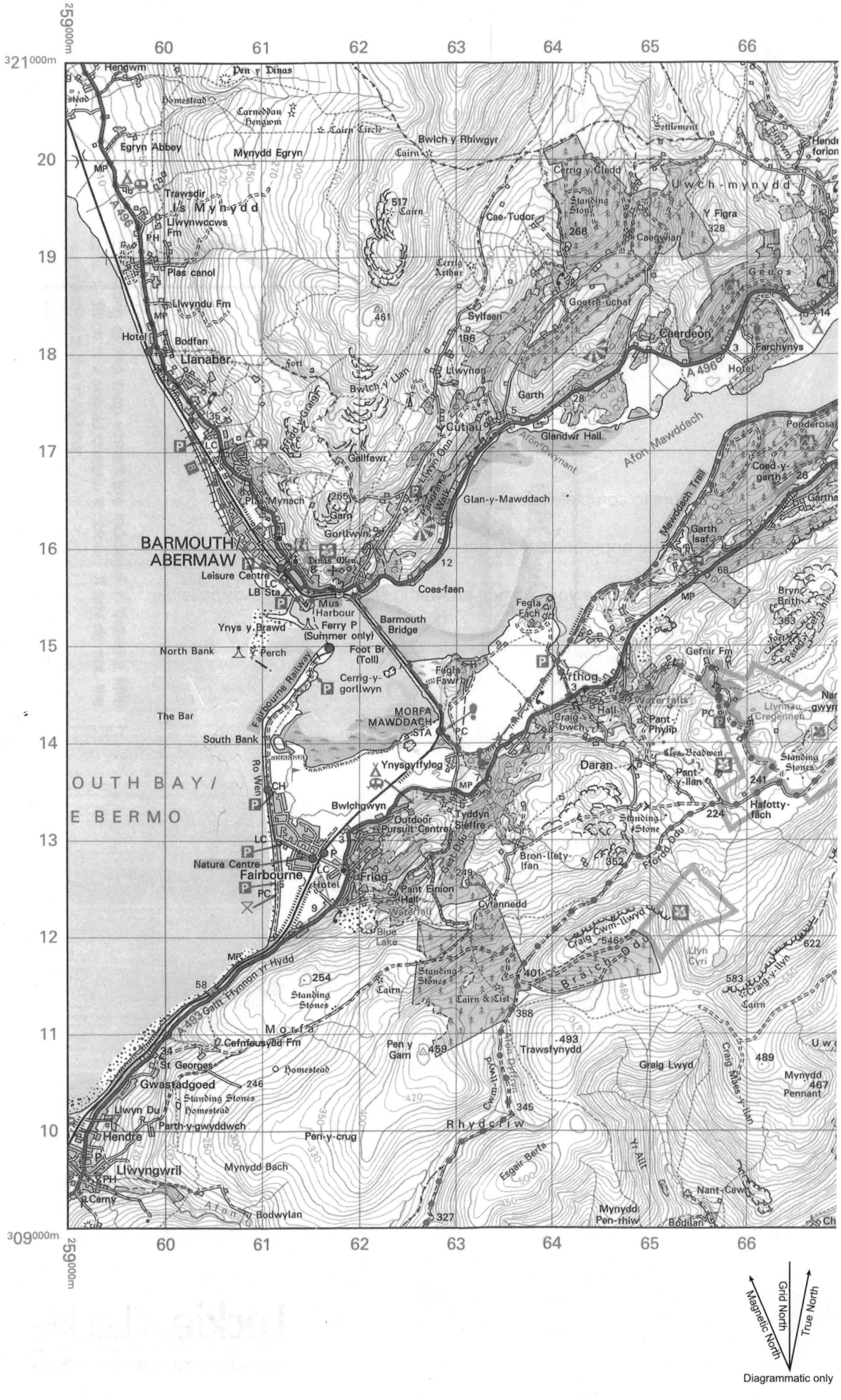

Four colours should appear above; if not then please return to the invigilator.
Four colours should appear above; if not then please return to the invigilator.

Extract No 1743/124

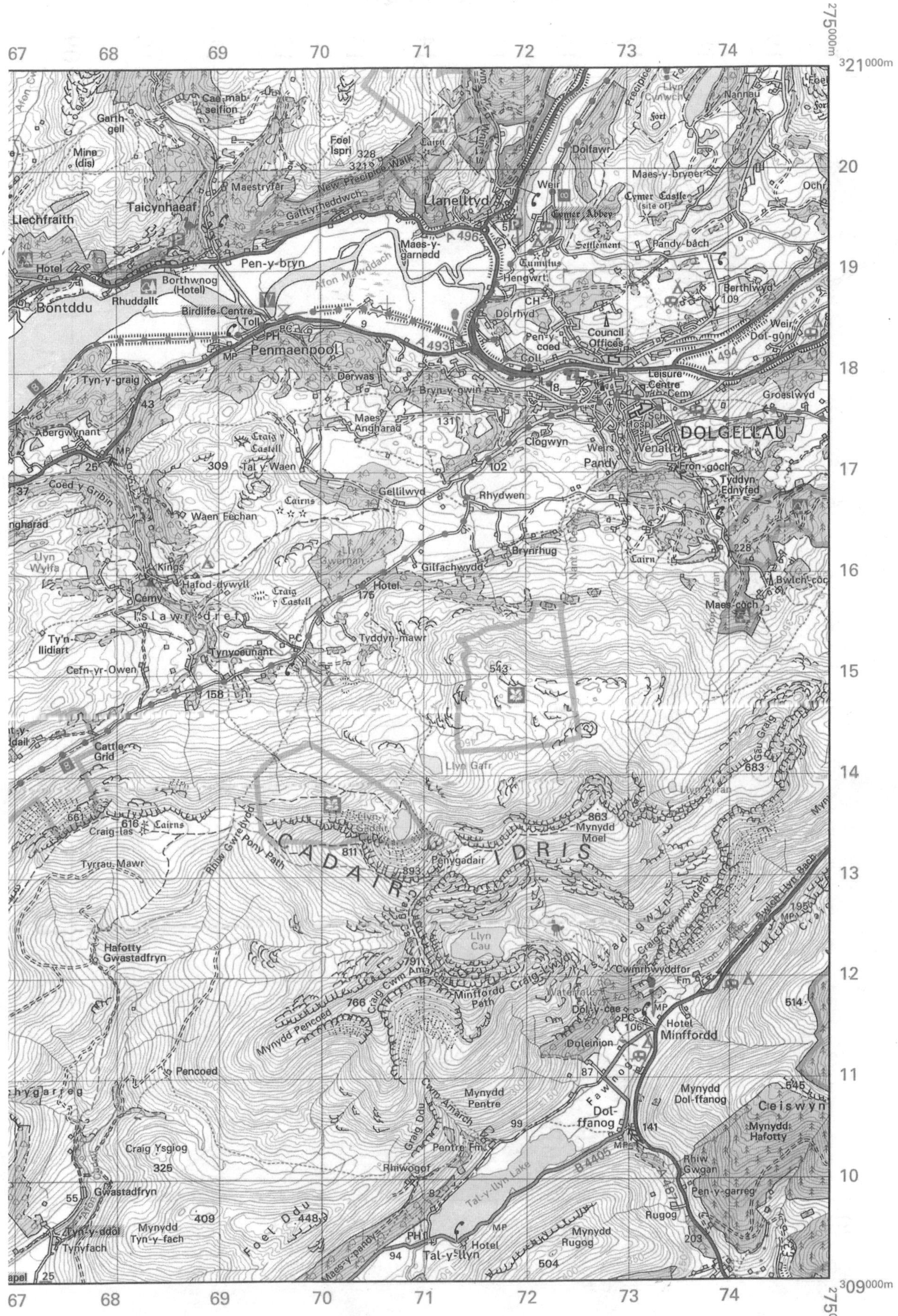

Scale 1:50 000

2 centimetres to 1 kilometre (one grid square)

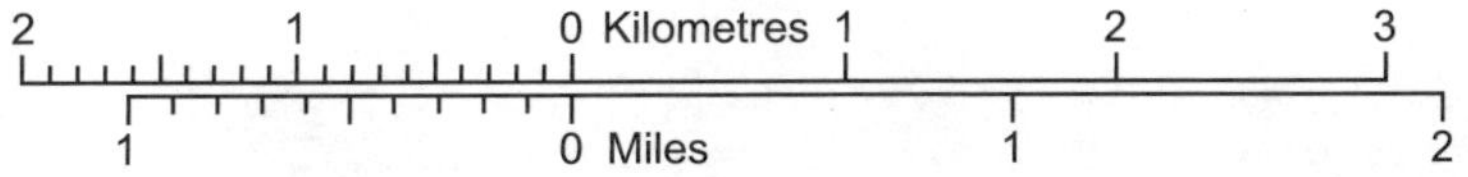

1 Kilometre = 0.6214 mile

1 mile = 1.6093 Kilometres

Reference Diagram Q1A

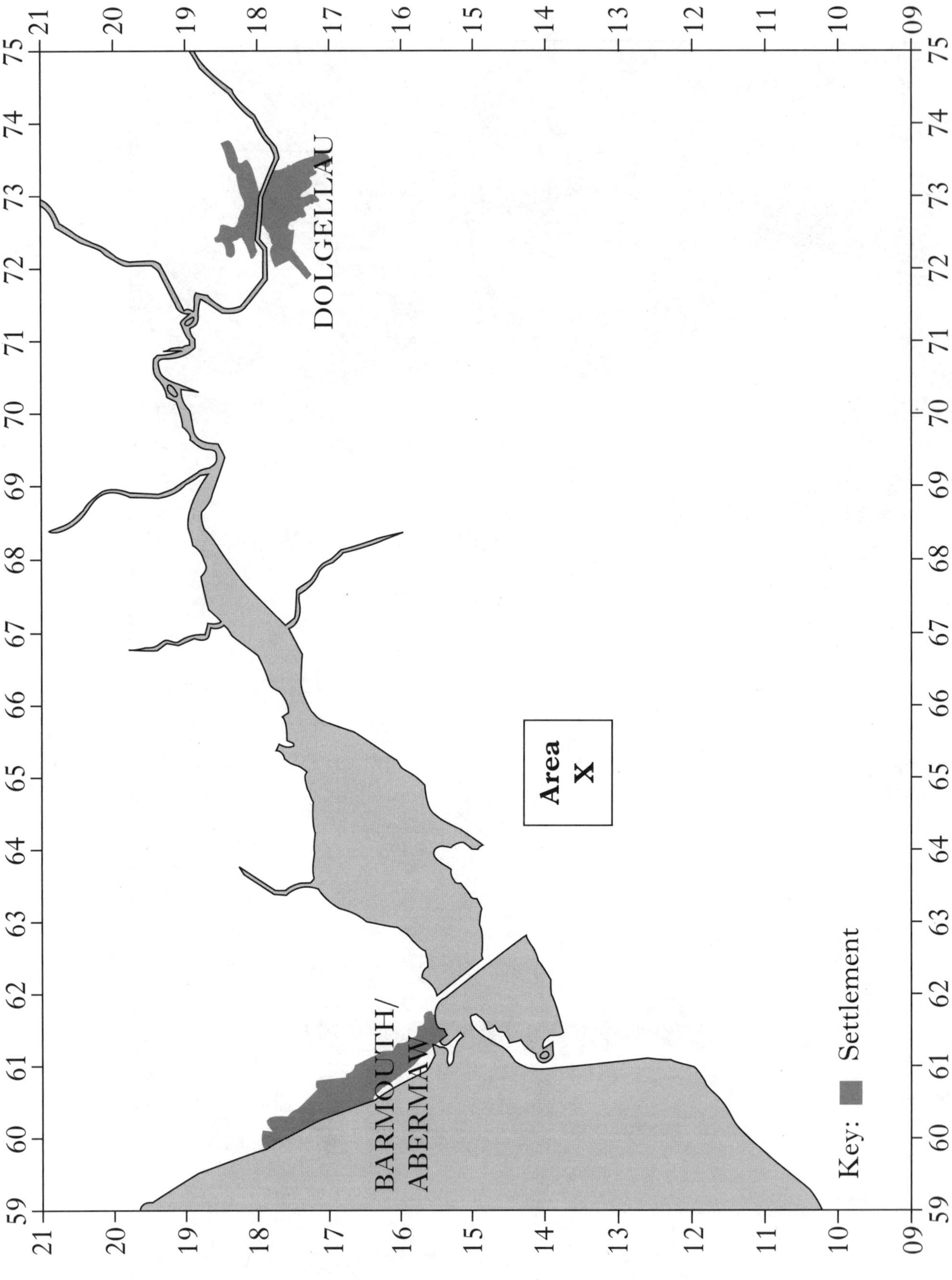

Marks

KU	ES

This question refers to the OS map extract of Barmouth and Reference Diagram Q1A.

1. (*a*) (i) Match each of the features named below with the correct grid reference.

Features: **u-shaped valley; corrie; pyramidal peak; arête**.

Choose from grid references:

709129 719119 710115 725106 — KU 3

(ii) **Explain** how a corrie is formed.

You may use diagram(s) to illustrate your answer. — KU 4

(*b*) Find Area X (6514) on Reference Diagram Q1A and the map extract.

Why is this area suitable for generating hydro-electric power? — KU 4

(*c*) The area covered by the map extract is popular with tourists.

Using map evidence, **describe** the advantages **and** disadvantages of this area for recreation and tourism. — ES 6

(*d*) Describe the **gathering techniques** which students could use to investigate the impact of tourism on the towns of Barmouth and Dollegellau.

Give reasons for your answer. — ES 5

(*e*) Why might there be **conflicts** between the various land uses in and around Barmouth? — ES 4

Marks KU ES

2. Reference Diagram Q2 14th March 2010.

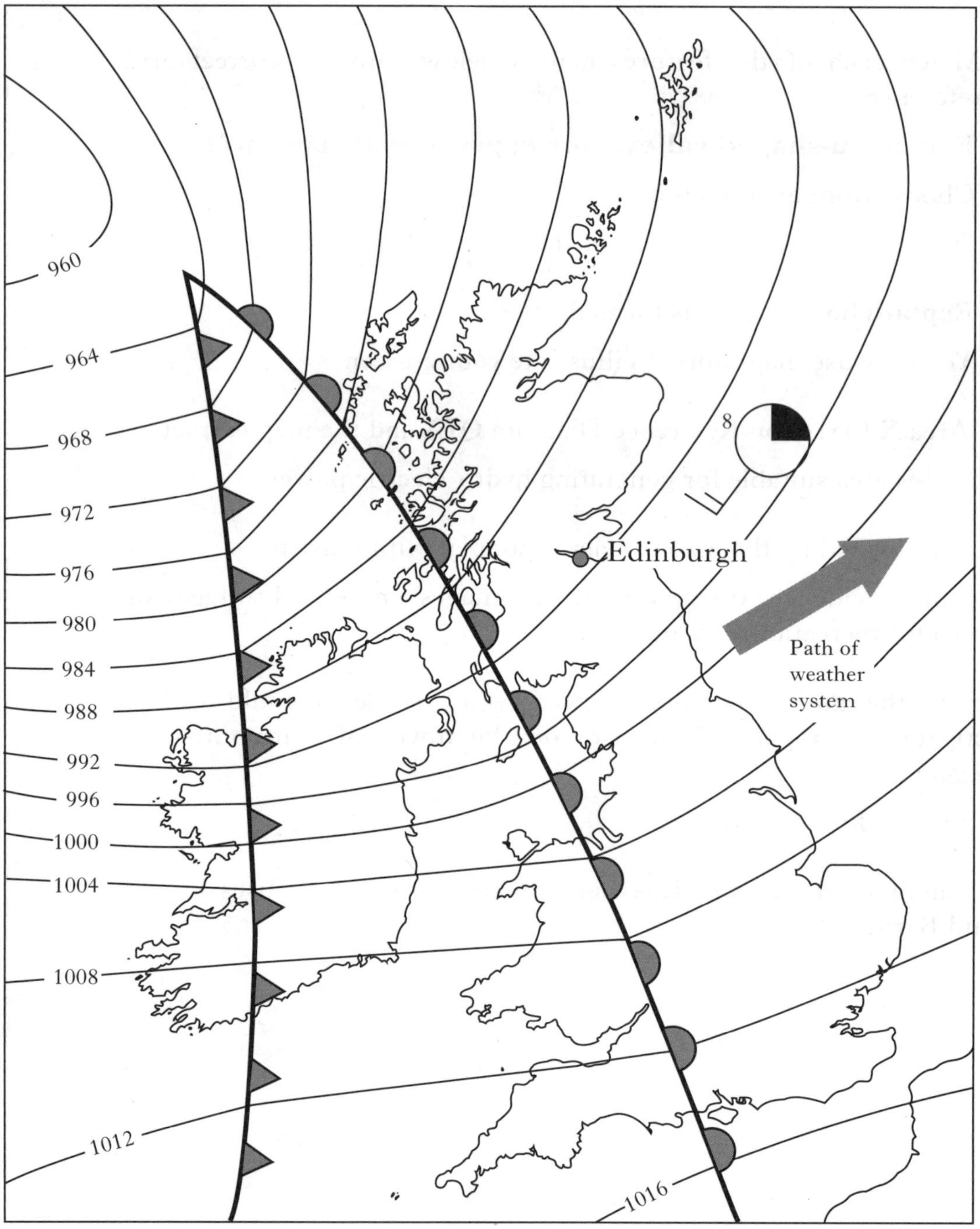

Study Reference Diagram Q2.

(*a*) Describe in detail the weather conditions being experienced in Edinburgh on Sunday 14th March 2010. **4**

(*b*) **Explain** the changes which will take place in Edinburgh over the next 24 hours. **6**

Marks

KU	ES
	6

3. Reference Diagram Q3A: Location map of UK off-shore wind farm zones.

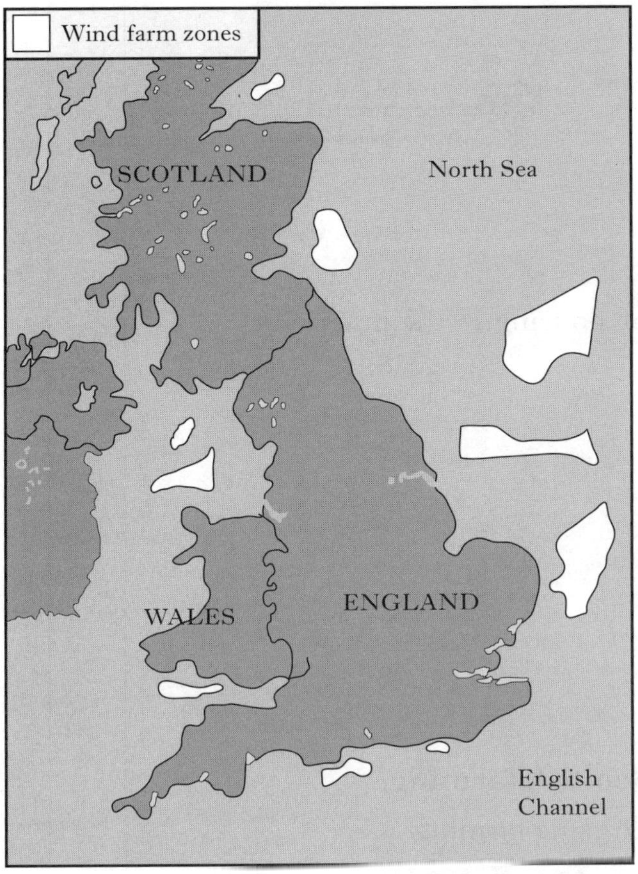

Reference Diagram Q3B: Off-shore wind farm and selected information.

- The UK's wind-swept coasts are ideal for off-shore turbines.
- £75 billion put into the UK's economy.
- Support up to 70,000 jobs by 2020.
- Cost £100 billion to build.
- Off-shore turbines are weather dependent.
- Turbines difficult to build and maintain in bad weather.

Reference Diagram Q3C: Statement from government spokesperson.

> A plan to generate enough electricity through off-shore wind farms to power millions of homes in the UK by 2020 has been approved by the Government. This green energy will replace electricity produced from non-renewable resources used in coal- and oil-fired power stations.

Study Reference Diagrams Q3A, Q3B and Q3C above.

'The benefits of the new off-shore wind turbines will outweigh the damage caused to the environment.'

To what extent do you agree with this statement?

Give reasons for your answer. **6**

Marks KU | ES

4. **Reference Diagram Q4: Urban Areas of a City.**

Study Reference Diagram Q4.

Explain in detail why there are different types of housing in the inner city and suburban areas of a city. KU 6

5. **Reference Diagram Q5: Recent changes in Scottish farming.**

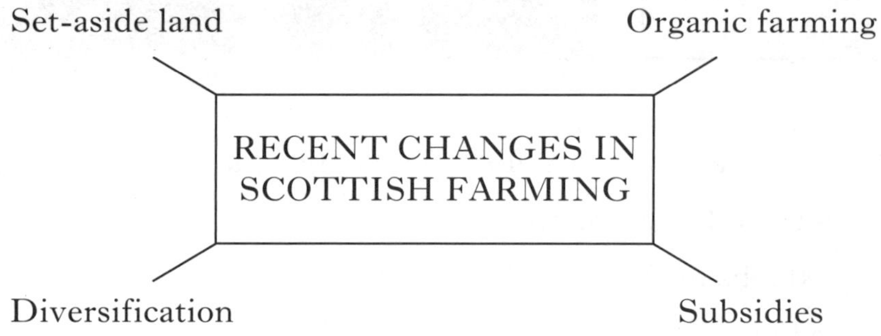

Choose **two** of the recent changes in farming and explain, in detail, why these bring both benefits and problems to the farmer. ES 5

Marks

KU	ES

6. Reference Diagram Q6A: Location map of Irn-Bru factory.

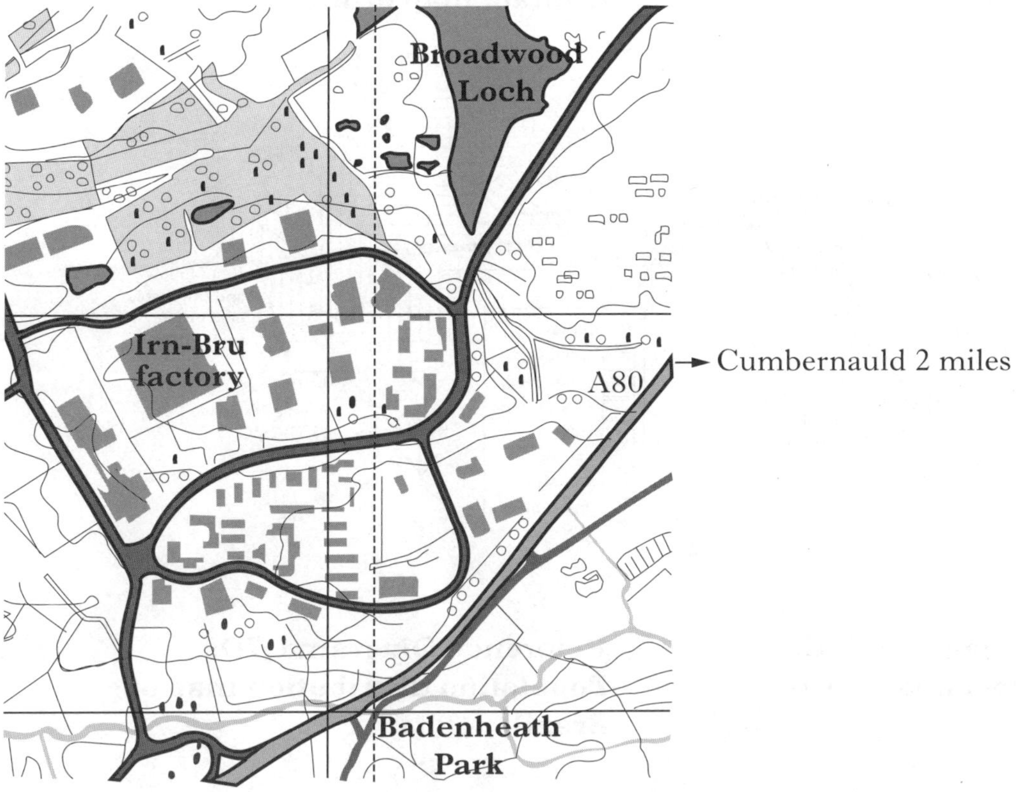

Reference Diagram Q6B: Site of Irn-Bru factory.

Study Reference Diagrams Q6A and Q6B.

Explain why the Irn-Bru factory is located in this area. **5** (ES)

Marks

KU	ES

7. Reference Diagram Q7A: Relief map of Brazil.

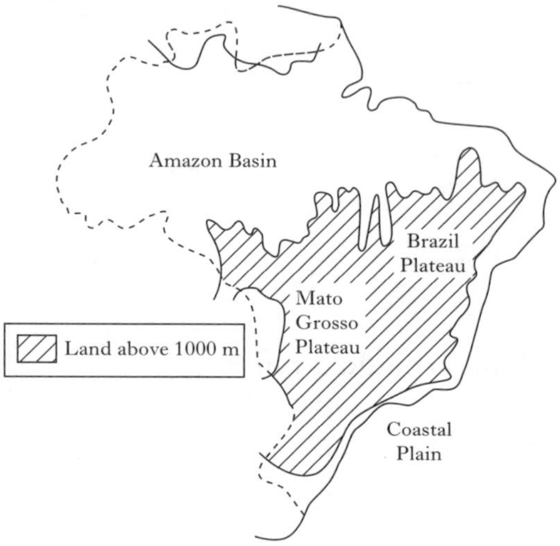

Reference Diagram Q7B: Climate map of Brazil.

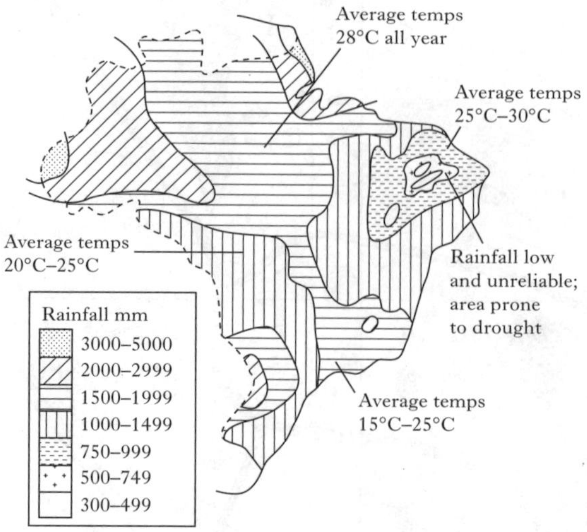

Reference Diagram Q7C: Industrial location map of Brazil.

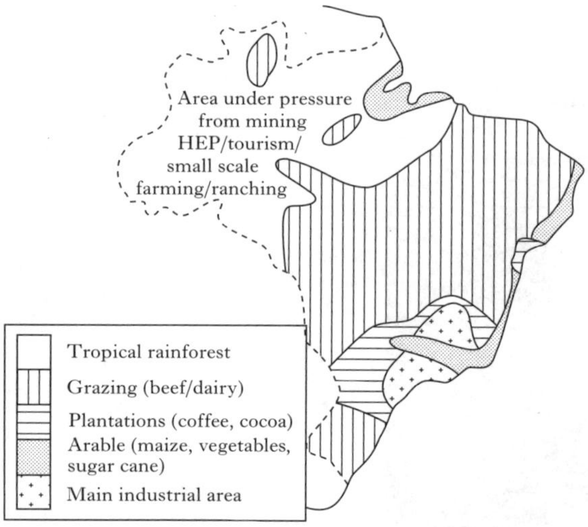

Reference Diagram Q7D: Population distribution map of Brazil.

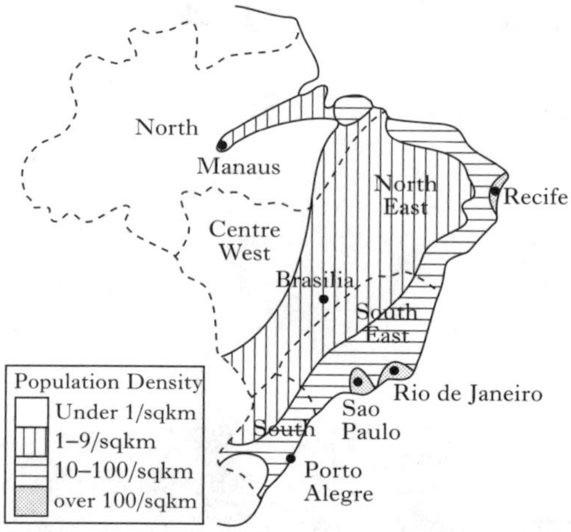

Study Reference Diagrams Q7A, Q7B, Q7C and Q7D.

Give reasons for the population distribution in Brazil. **4**

Marks	
KU	ES

8. Reference Diagram Q8A: Demographic Transition Model.

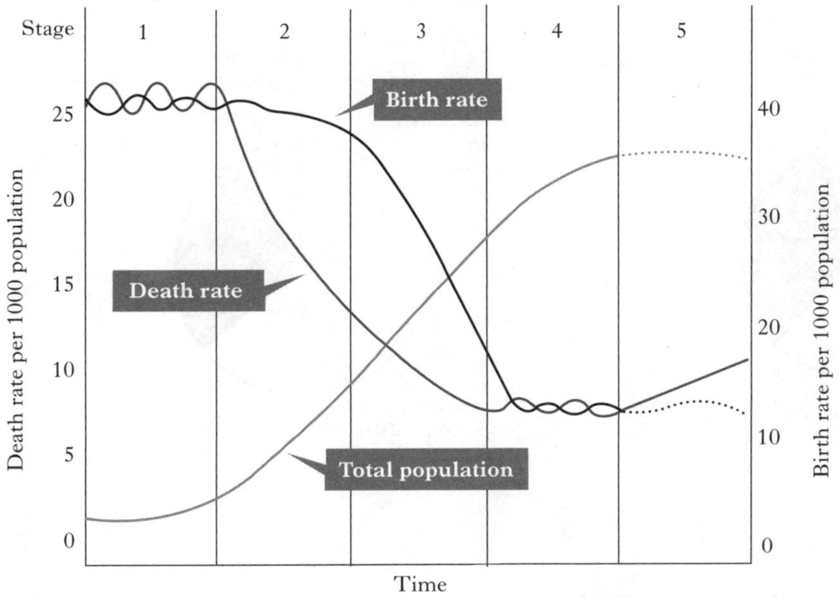

Reference Diagram Q8B: Birth Rates and Death Rates for India.

Year	Birth Rate per 1,000 People	Death Rate per 1,000 People
1970	38	16
1990	32	10
2007	23	8

Study Reference Diagrams Q8A and Q8B.

(*a*) The Demographic Transition Model has 5 stages. At which stage was India at in 2007?

Give reasons for your answer. **4** (ES)

(*b*) **Explain** ways in which developing countries, such as India are reducing birth rates. **5** (KU)

Marks

KU	ES

9. Reference Diagram Q9A: Imports to the USA 2008.

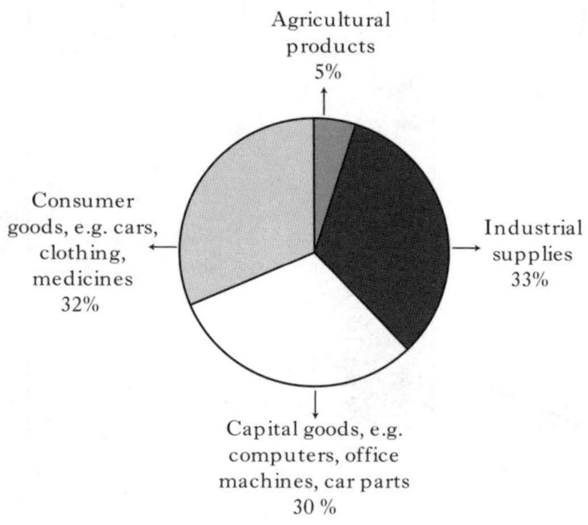

Reference Diagram Q9B: Exports from the USA 2008.

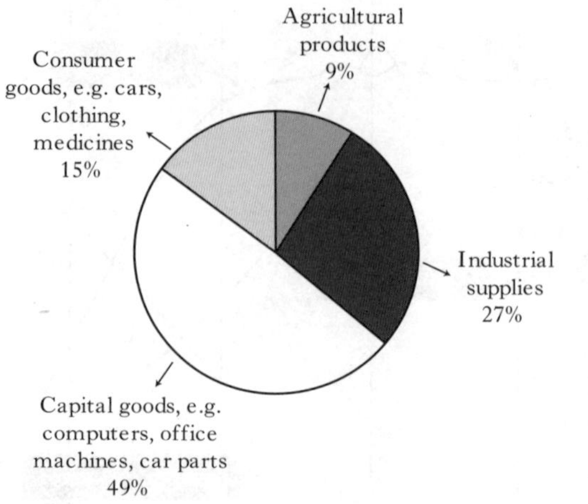

(*a*) Study Reference Diagrams Q9A and Q9B.

Describe the main differences between the USA's imports and exports. **4**

(*b*) Describe other **processing** techniques that could be used to display the information in Reference Diagrams Q9A and Q9B.

Give reasons for your choice of techniques. **5**

General Level Exam B

Geography

Standard Grade: General Level

Practice Papers
For SQA Exams

General Level
Exam B

Fill in these boxes:

Name of centre

Town

Forename(s)

Surname

You are allowed 1 hour, 25 minutes to complete this paper.

Make sure you read the questions carefully.

Try to answer all of the questions in the time allowed.

Write your answers in the space provided.

Make sure you write as neatly as you can and answer in sentences wherever possible.

Where required insert a tick ✓ in the box ☐ beside the correct answer.

Leckie × Leckie
Scotland's leading educational publishers

1:50 000 Scale
Landranger Series

Extract No 1656/104

Four colours should appear above; if not then please return to the invigilator.

Four colours should appear above; if not then please return to the invigilator.

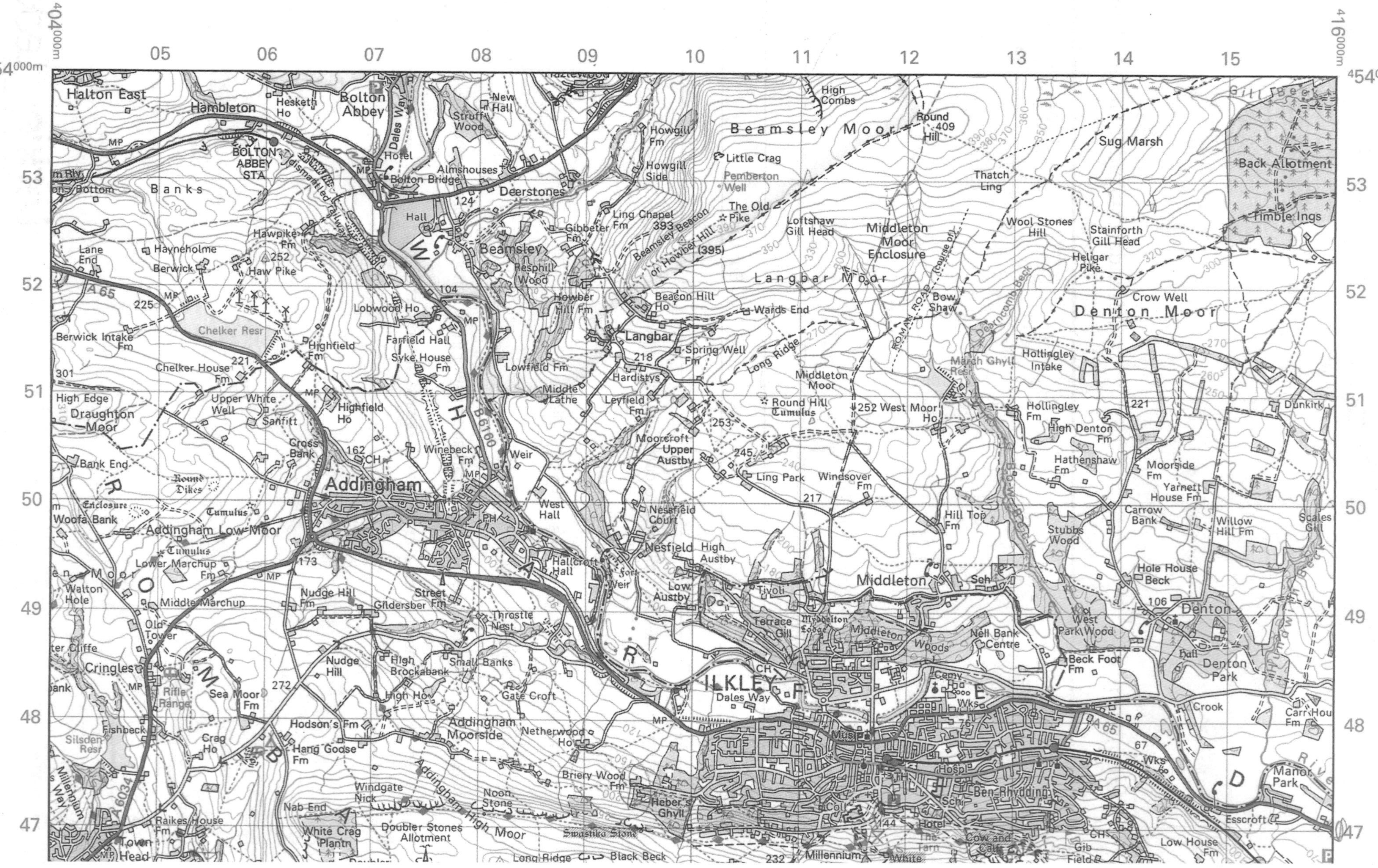

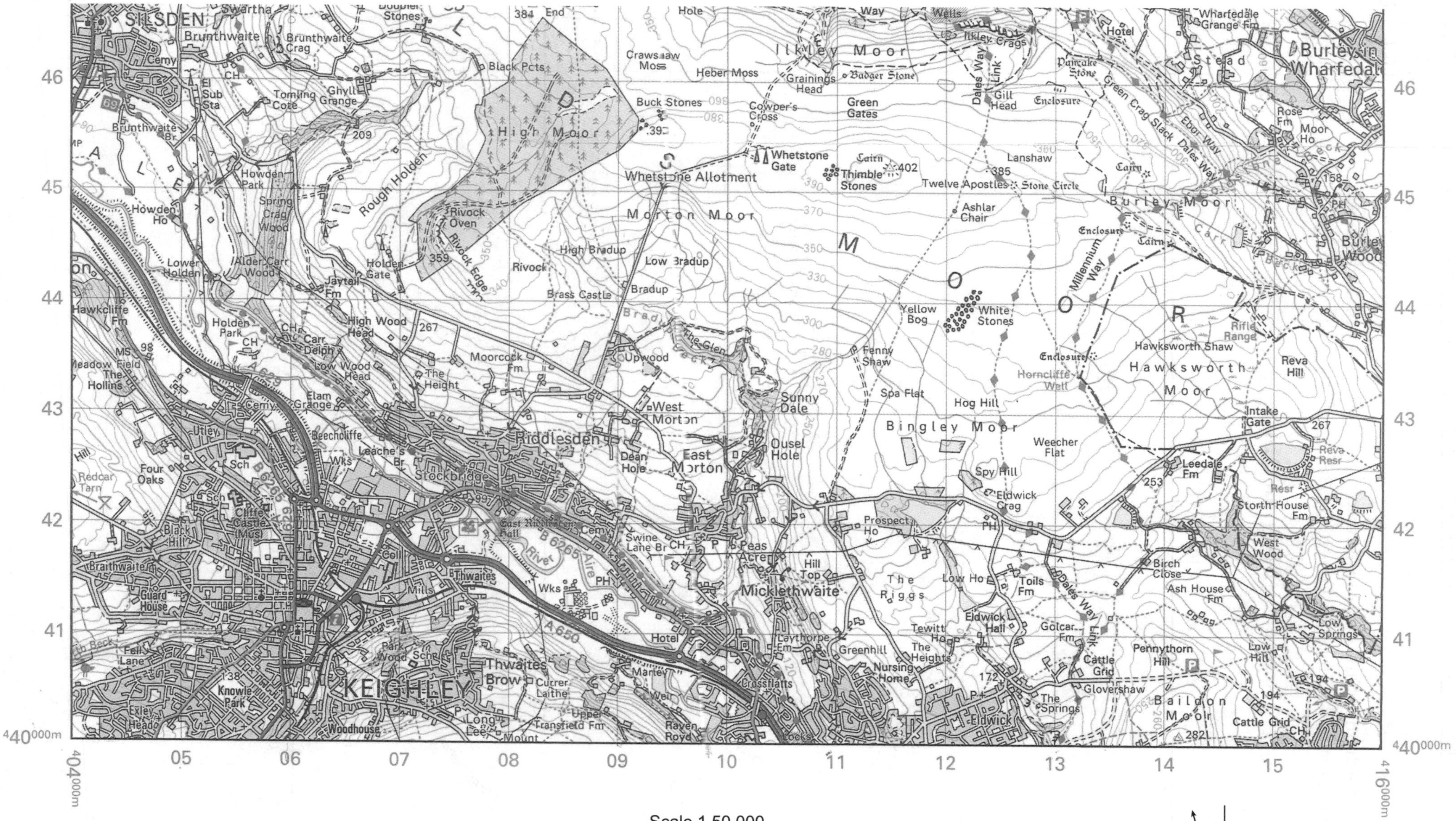
SILSDEN
Brunthwaite
Bunthwaite Crag
Tomling Cote
Ghyll Grange
Howden Park
Spring Crag Wood
Howden Ho
Lower Holden
Alder Carr Wood
Rough Holden
Rivock Oven
Rivock Edge
Holden Gate
Jaytail Fm
Black Pcts
High Moor
Craws Law Moss
Heber Moss
Buck Stones
Cowper's Cross
Whetstone Gate
Whetstone Allotment
Morton Moor
High Bradup
Low Bradup
Bradup
Rivock
Brass Castle
Ilkley Moor
Badger Stone
Graining Head
Green Gates
Thimble Stones
Twelve Apostles
Stone Circle
Lanshaw
Ashlar Chair
Gill Head
Dales Way Link
Ilkley Crags
Wells
Hotel
Pancake Stone
Green Crag Slack
Ebor Way
Dales Way
Wharfedale Grange Fm
Stead
Burley-in-Wharfedale
Rose Fm
Moor Ho
Burley Moor
Burley Wood
Enclosure
Cairn
Millennium Way
Yellow Bog
White Stones
Hawksworth Shaw
Hawksworth Moor
Horncliffe Well
Rifle Range
Reva Hill
Intake Gate
Reva Resr
Fenny Shaw
Spa Flat
Hog Hill
Bingley Moor
Weecher Flat
Spy Hill
Eldwick Crag
Leedale Fm
Storth House Fm
West Wood
Birch Close
Ash House Fm
Low Springs
Hawkcliffe Fm
Meadow Field
The Hollins
Holden Park
Carr Delph
Low Wood Head
High Wood Head
Elam Grange
Beechcliffe
Leache's Br
Stockbridge
Moorcock Fm
The Height
Riddlesden
Upwood
West Morton
Dean Hole
East Morton
Sunny Dale
Ousel Hole
The Glen
Utley
Four Oaks
Redcar Tarn
Cliffe Castle (Mus)
Black Hill
Braithwaite
Guard House
Fell Lane
Knowle Park
Exley Head
KEIGHLEY
Woodhouse
Thwaites
Thwaites Brow
Currer Laithe
Upper Transfield Fm
Long Lee
Mount
Park Wood
East Riddlesden Hall
River Aire
Swine Lane Br
Peas Acre
Hill Top
Micklethwaite
Prospect Ho
The Riggs
Low Ho
Toils Fm
Eldwick Hall
Golcar Fm
Tewitt Hall
The Heights
Nursing Home
Greenhill
Laythorpe Fm
Crossflatts
Hotel
Marley
Raven Royd
Eldwick
The Springs
Cattle Grid
Glovershaw
Pennythorn Hill
Baildon Moor
Low Hill
B 6265
A 629
A 650
440000m
404000m
416000m
05
06
07
08
09
10
11
12
13
14
15
41
42
43
44
45
46

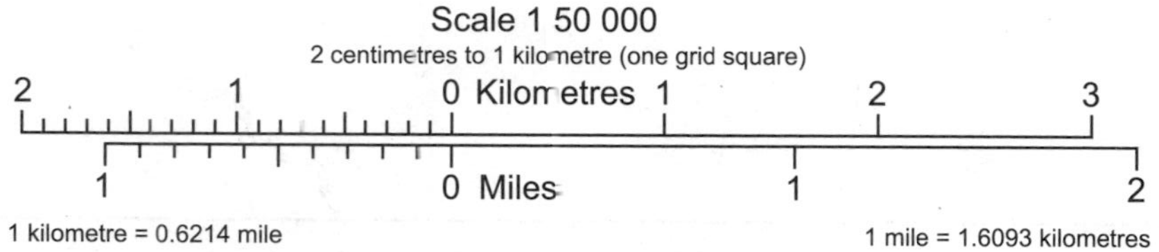
Scale 1 50 000
2 centimetres to 1 kilometre (one grid square)
Kilometres
2
1
0
1
2
3
Miles
1
0
1
2
1 kilometre = 0.6214 mile
1 mile = 1.6093 kilometres

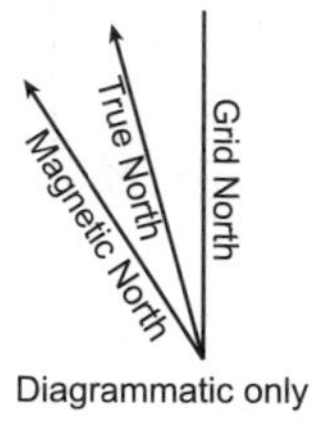
Grid North
True North
Magnetic North
Diagrammatic only

DO NOT WRITE IN THIS MARGIN

Marks | KU | ES

1. Look at the Ordnance Survey Map Extract [No. 1656/140] of Ilkley and its surrounding area and Reference Diagram Q1A.

Reference Diagram Q1A

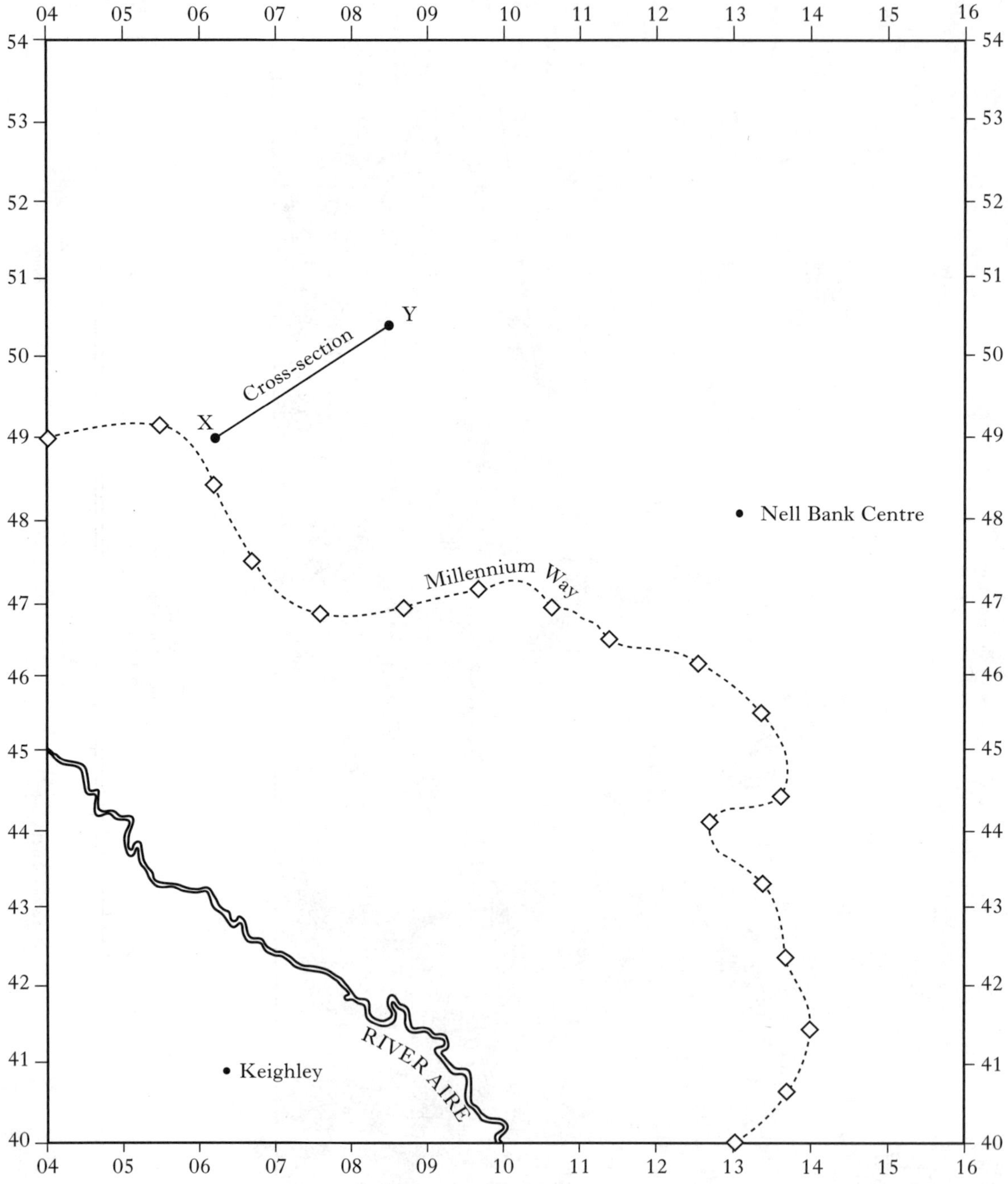

DO NOT WRITE IN THIS MARGIN

Marks | KU | ES

(*a*) **Reference Diagram Q1B: Cross-section from 063490 to 096502**

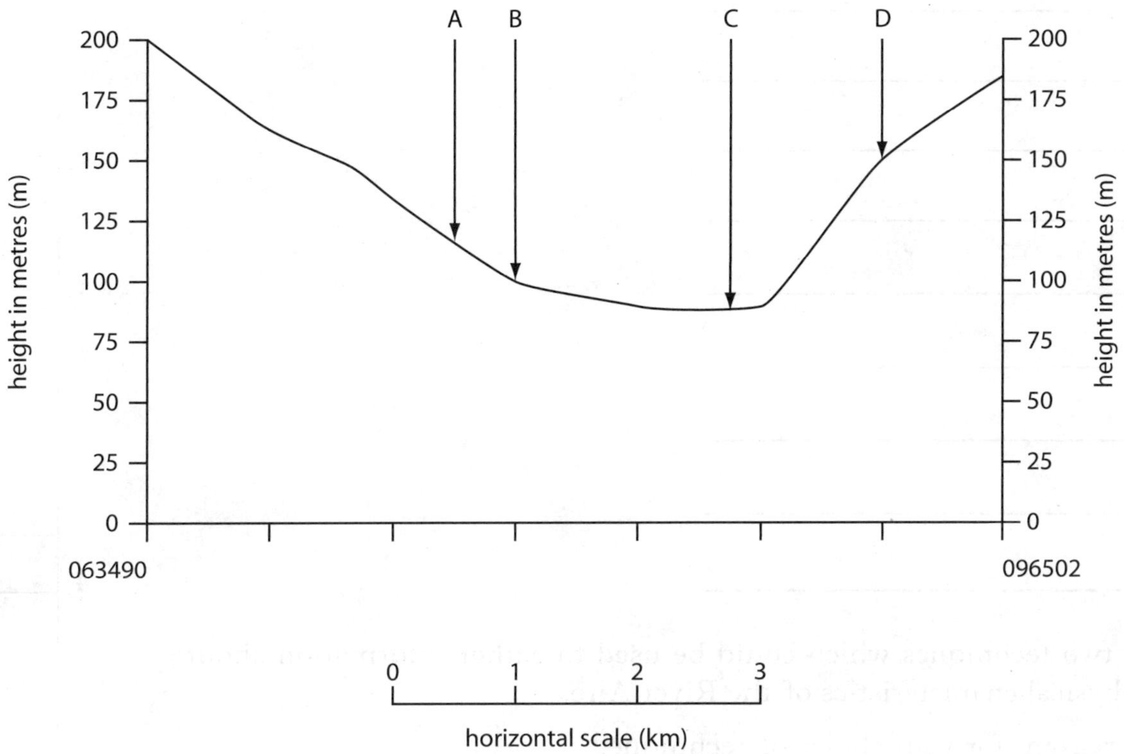

1. (continued)

Look at cross-section X–Y on Reference Diagrams Q1A and Q1B and the map extract.

Identify the features A, B, C, and D by writing the correct letter in the table below.

Feature on map	Letter
Outskirts of Addingham	
Primary road	
Woodland	
River	

3

DO NOT WRITE IN THIS MARGIN

Marks KU ES

(*b*) Explain why an ox-bow lake is likely to develop in grid square 0841.

You may use diagrams to illustrate your answer.

____

____

____

____

____

____

____

____

____

______________________________ **4**

(*c*) Give two techniques which could be used to gather information about the physical characteristics of the River Aire.

Give reasons for your choice of technique.

Technique 1 ______________________________

Reason ______________________________

____

Technique 2 ______________________________

Reason ______________________________

______________________________ **4**

DO NOT WRITE IN THIS MARGIN

1. (continued)

Marks | KU | ES

(*d*) Nell Bank Centre at 127487 is an outdoor education centre* for school pupils.

(*this type of centre offers pupils instruction in outdoor activities and provides fieldwork experiences outwith the classroom)

How good is this location for the centre?

Give reasons for your answer.

____

____

____

____

____ 4

(*e*) Find the Millennium Way footpath on Reference Diagram Q1A and the Ordnance Survey Map.

The Millennium Way is part of a long distance footpath for recreational walkers.

Using map evidence, what are the advantages and disadvantages of this route?

____

____

____

____

____ 4

DO NOT WRITE IN THIS MARGIN

Marks	KU	ES

1. (continued)

(*f*) Give map evidence to show that the CBD of Keighley is located in grid square 0641.

____

____

____

______________________________ **4**

2. Reference Diagram Q2: Features of Glacial Deposition.

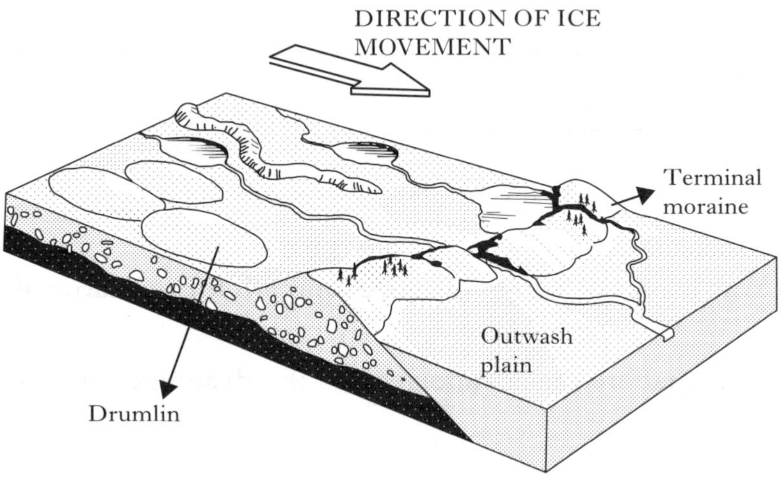

Look at Reference Diagram Q2.

Choose one of the named features above and **explain** how it was formed.

You may use diagram(s) to illustrate your answer.

____

____

____

____

____

____

______________________________ **3**

DO NOT WRITE IN THIS MARGIN

Marks | KU | ES

3\. (*a*) **Reference Diagram Q3A: Possible Sites for a Weather Station.**

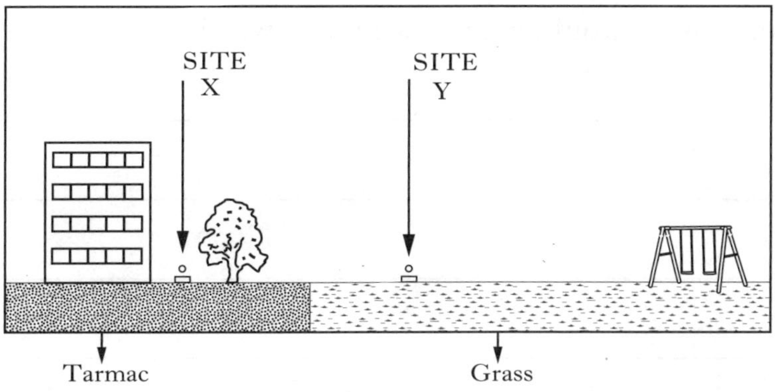

Look at Reference Diagram Q3A

Do you think that site X or Y is the better site for a weather station?

Tick (✓) your choice. X ☐ Y ☐

Give reasons for your choice.

____

____

____

____

____ 3

(*b*) **Reference Diagram Q3B: The 5 Main Air Masses Affecting Britain.**

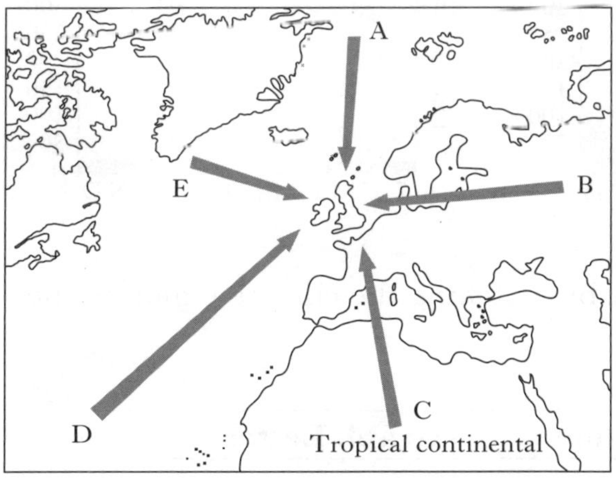

(i) Describe the type of weather Britain might experience with air mass A.

____

____

____ 2

DO NOT WRITE IN THIS MARGIN

3. (continued)

Marks | KU | ES

(ii) Explain why air mass C would bring warm, dry weather.

______

______

______

______ 2

4. (*a*) Reference Diagram Q4A: Climate Graphs.

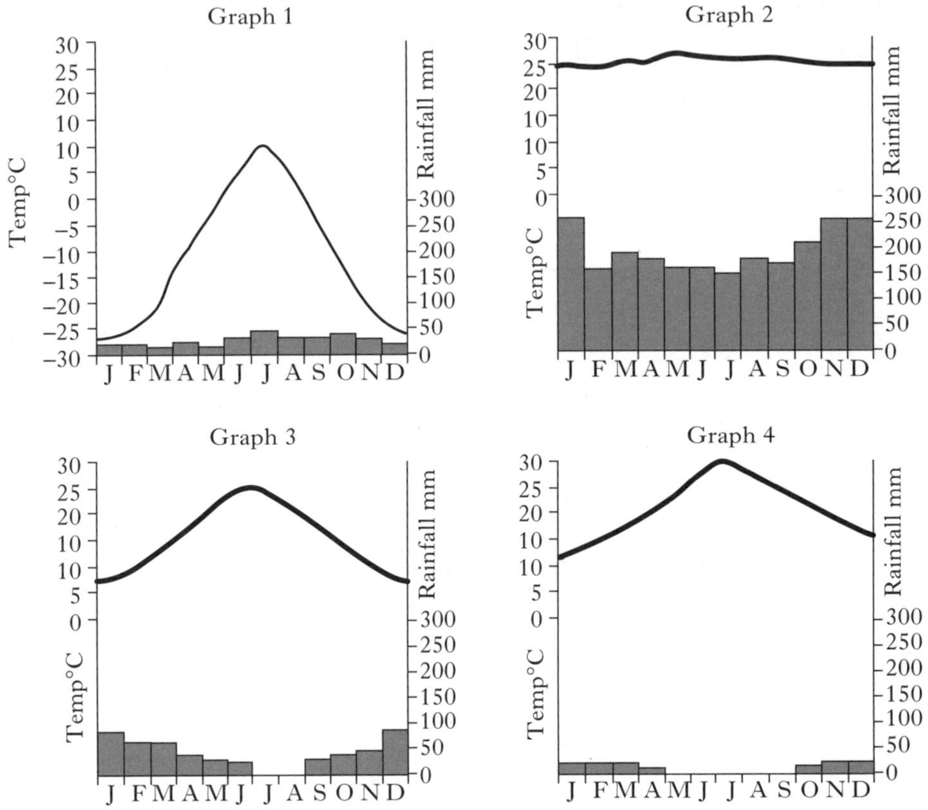

Complete the table below by matching the climate region to the correct graph.

Climate Region	**Graph Letter**
Equatorial Rain Forest	
Tundra	
Mediterranean	
Hot Desert	

3

DO NOT WRITE IN THIS MARGIN

Marks KU ES

4. (continued)

(*b*) What are the likely advantages and disadvantages for people living in areas which have the climate shown in **Graph 3?**

Advantages ______________________________

____

____

Disadvantages ______________________________

____

______________________________ **4**

5. Reference Diagram Q5A: Land affected by desertification worldwide.

Continent	**% of total area affected by desertification**
Africa	37
Asia	34
North America	11
South America	8
Oceania	7
Europe	3

(*a*) Study Diagram Q5A.

Complete the divided bar graph below.

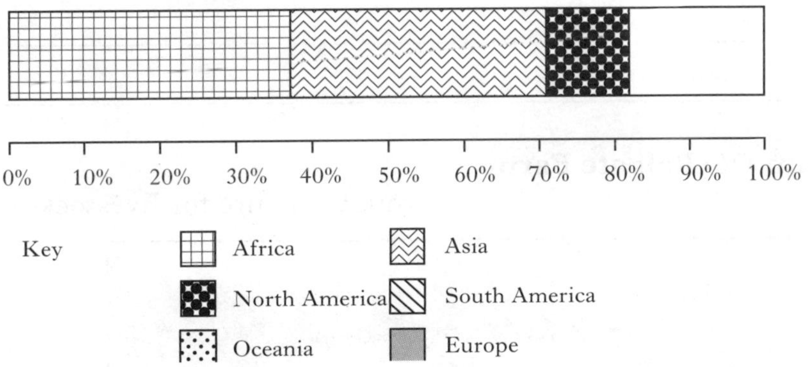

3

DO NOT WRITE IN THIS MARGIN

(*b*) **Reference Diagram Q5B: Possible Solutions to Desertification.**

Marks | KU | ES

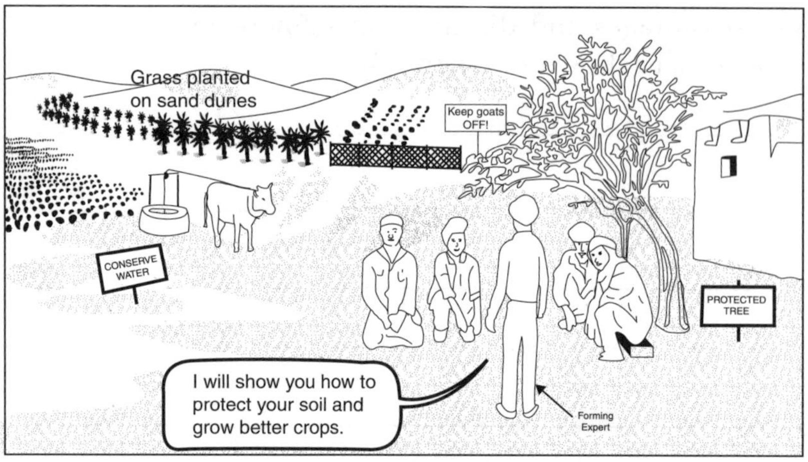

5. (continued)

Study Diagram Q5B which shows possible methods of slowing down the spread of deserts.

Choose any two of these solutions and explain fully how they would slow down desertification.

Solution 1 ______________________________

Reasons ______________________________

____

Solution 2 ______________________________

Reasons ______________________________

______________________________ **4**

6. Reference Diagram Q6: Belgate Farm

July temperature: 16°C
December temperature: -2°C
Annual rainfall: 1020 mm

DO NOT WRITE IN THIS MARGIN

Marks | KU | ES

Study Reference Diagram Q6 on page 54.

'Mixed farming is the most suitable type of farming for Belgate farm.'

Tick (✓) your choice. Yes ☐ No ☐

Give reasons for your choice.

____

____

____

____ **4**

7. Reference Diagram Q7: Service Sector employment in selected countries.

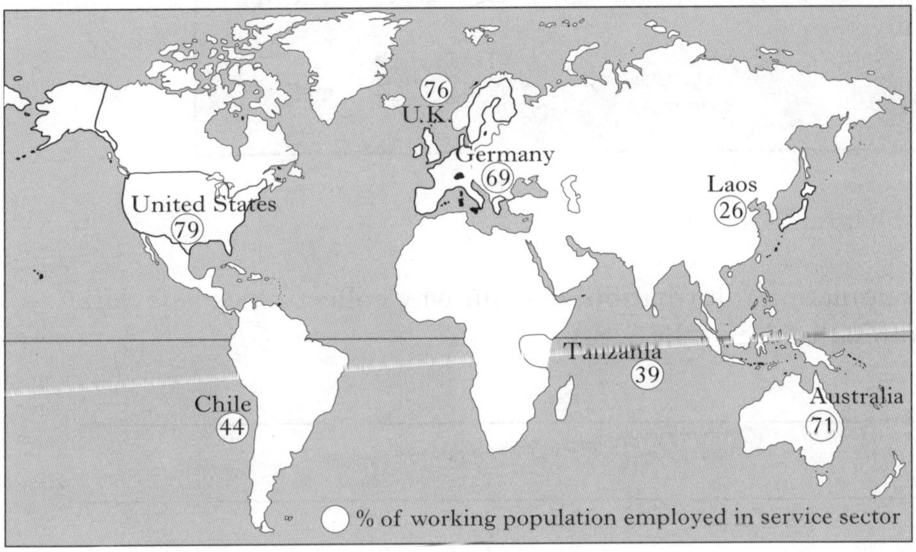

Give other processing techniques that could be used to display the information shown on the above map.

Give reasons for you choice of techniques.

____

____

____

____ **4**

DO NOT WRITE IN THIS MARGIN

8. Reference Diagram Q8: Differences between USA and Haiti.

Marks | KU | ES

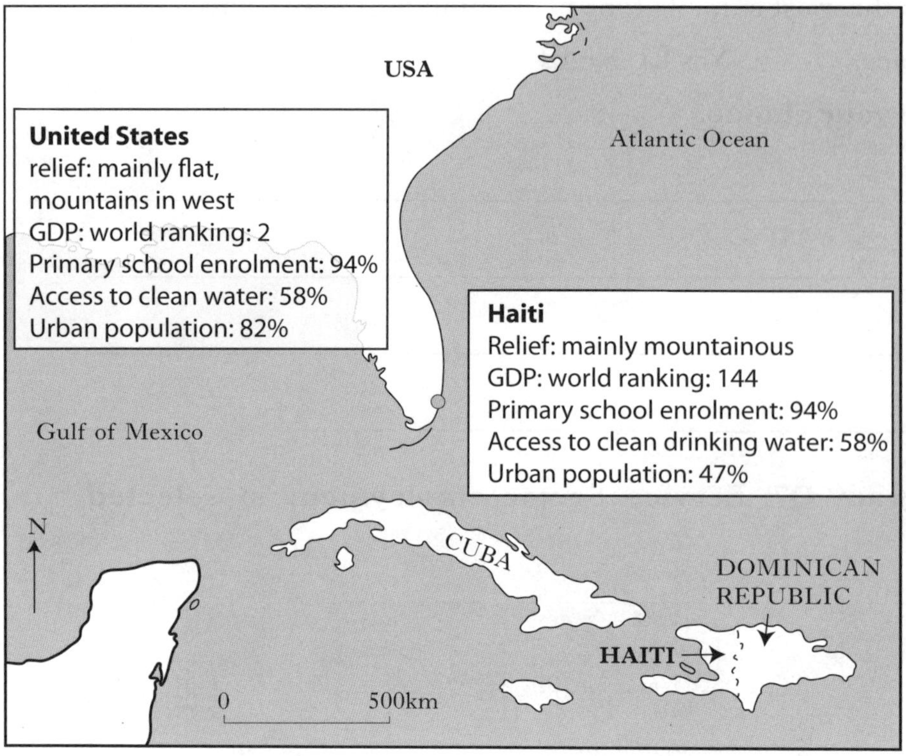

Study Reference Diagram Q8.

Referring to the population information, explain why collecting census data in Haiti is more difficult than in the USA.

____

____

____

____ **4**

DO NOT WRITE IN THIS MARGIN

Marks | KU | ES

9. (*a*) **Reference Diagram Q9A: World Price of Coffee.**

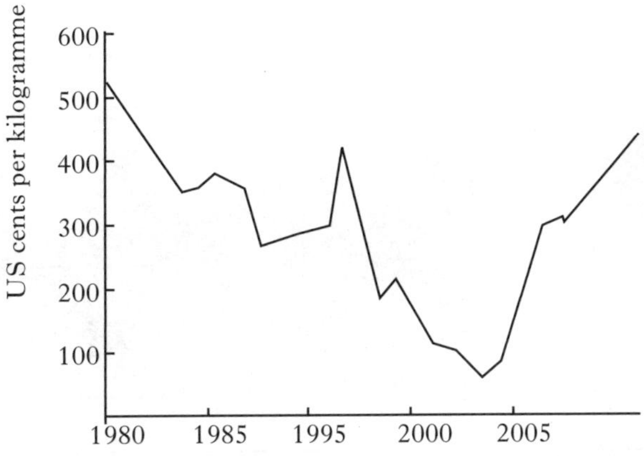

Describe the changes in the price of coffee since 1980.

______

______

______ **3**

(*b*) **Reference Diagram Q9B: Uganda's Exports and Imports.**

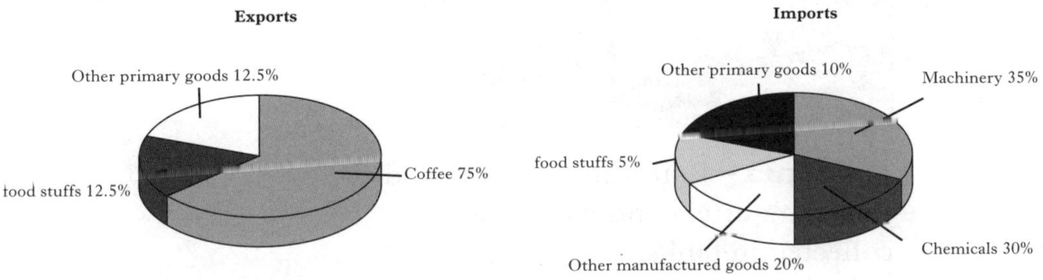

"If Uganda's coffee harvest failed it would be a disaster for the country."

Do you fully agree with this statement?

Give reasons for your answer.

______

______

______

______ **4**

DO NOT WRITE IN THIS MARGIN

10. Reference Diagram Q10: Examples of Intermediate Technology from around the World.

Marks | KU | ES

Sudan – Fuel efficient stoves use 50% less firewood.

Nepal – Bicycle ambulances transport the sick from remote villages to the nearest town.

Tanzania – Rainwater is harvested through gutters and pipes and collected in tanks.

Study Reference Diagram Q10.

Explain why such types of intermediate technology are most appropriate for developing countries.

4

Credit Level Exam B

Geography

Standard Grade: Credit Level

Practice Papers
For SQA Exams

Credit Level
Exam B

You are allowed 2 hours to complete this paper.

Marks will be allocated for appropriate sketches and diagrams.

Make sure you write as neatly as you can and answer in sentences wherever possible.

Leckie × Leckie
Scotland's leading educational publishers

1:50 000 Scale
Landranger Series

Extract No 1656/104

Four colours should appear above; if not then please return to the invigilator.

Four colours should appear above; if not then please return to the invigilator.

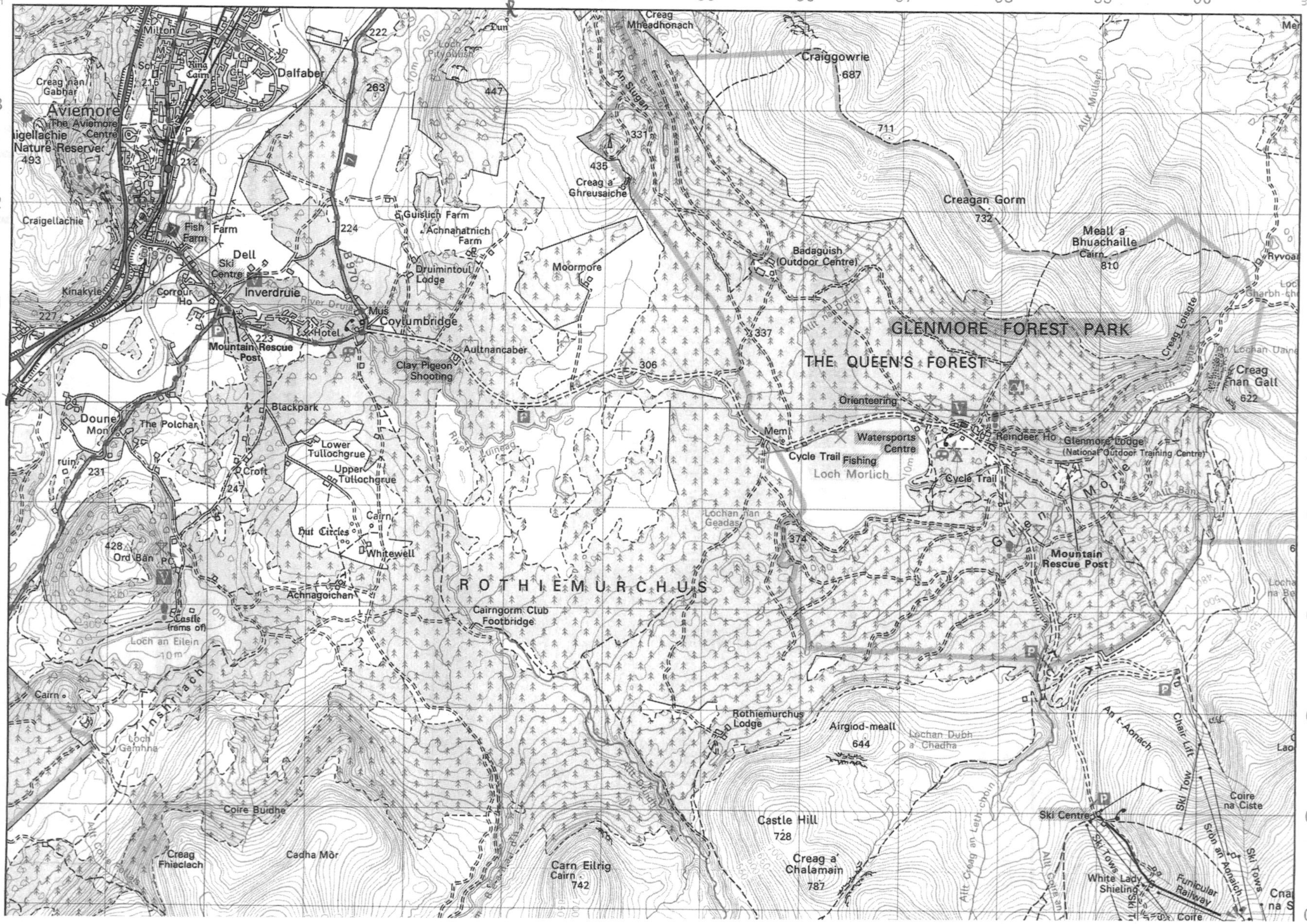

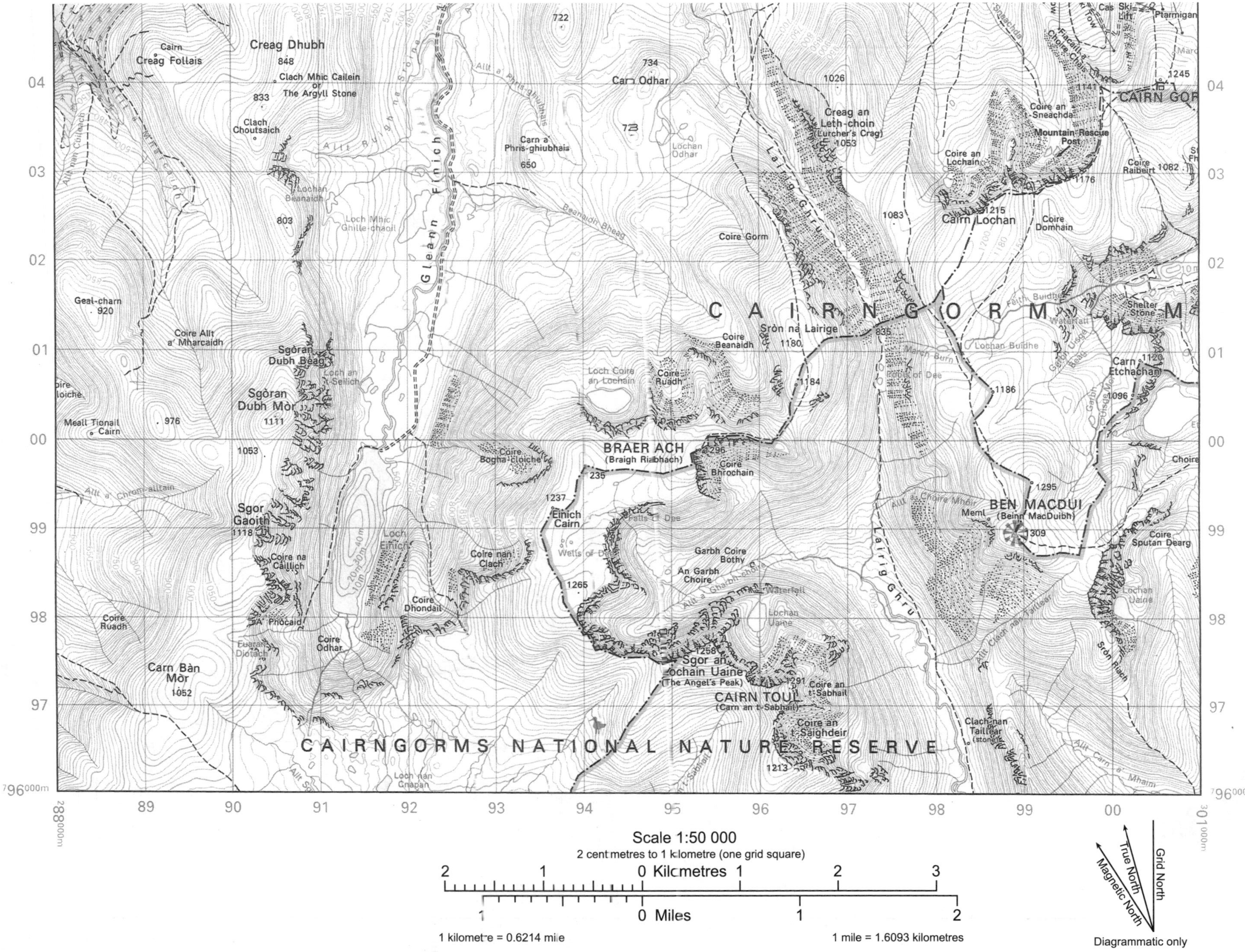
CAIRNGORM
CAIRNGORMS NATIONAL NATURE RESERVE
Creag Dhubh
Cairn Creag Follais
Clach Mhic Cailein or The Argyll Stone
Clach Choutsaich
Carn Odhar
Carn a' Phris-ghiubhais
Lochan Odhar
Creag an Leth-choin (Lurcher's Crag)
Coire an t-Sneachda
Mountain Rescue Post
Coire an Lochain
Cairn Lochan
Coire Domhain
Coire Raibeirt
CAIRN GOR
Ptarmigan
Lairig Ghru
Coire Gorm
Loch Mhic Ghille-chaoil
Lochan Beanaidh
Gleann Einich
Geal-charn
Coire Allt a' Mharcaidh
Sgòran Dubh Beag
Sgòran Dubh Mòr
Loch an t-Seilich
Meall Tionail Cairn
Sròn na Lairige
Coire Beanaidh
Loch Coire an Lochain
Coire Ruadh
Lochan Buidhe
Shelter Stone
Carn Etchachan
BRAERIACH (Braigh Riabhach)
Coire Bhrochain
Coire Bogha-cloiche
Einich Cairn
Wells of Dee
Falls of Dee
Pools of Dee
March Burn
Garbh Coire Bothy
An Garbh Choire
Waterfall
Lochan Uaine
BEN MACDUI (Beinn MacDuibh)
Coire Sputan Dearg
Lochan Uaine
Sròn Riach
Sgor Gaoith
Coire na Caillich
Loch Einich
Coire nan Clach
Coire Dhondail
Coire Ruadh
A' Phocaid
Coire Odhar
Carn Bàn Mòr
Sgor an Lochain Uaine (The Angel's Peak)
CAIRN TOUL (Carn an t-Sabhail)
Coire an t-Sabhail
Coire an t-Saighdeir
Clach nan Taillear (stone)
Loch nan Cnapan
04
03
02
01
00
99
98
97
796000m
288000m
89
90
91
92
93
94
95
96
97
98
99
00
301000m
Scale 1:50 000
2 centimetres to 1 kilometre (one grid square)
2 1 0 Kilometres 1 2 3
1 0 Miles 1 2
1 kilometre = 0.6214 mile
1 mile = 1.6093 kilometres
Grid North
True North
Magnetic North
Diagrammatic only

Reference Diagram Q1A: The Aviemore Area

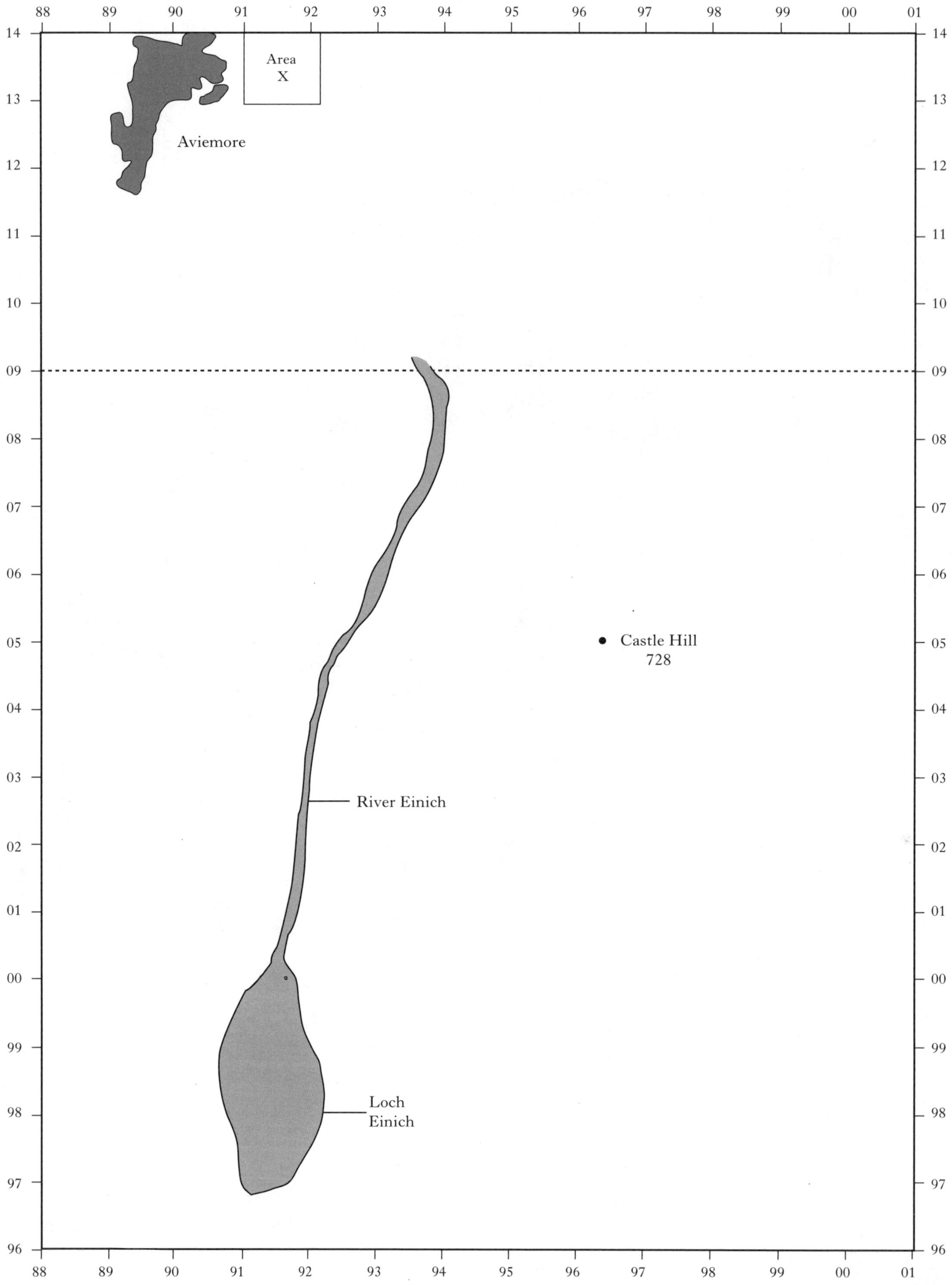

Marks

KU | ES

This question refers to the OS map extract of the Aviemore area and Reference Diagram Q1A.

1. (*a*) Describe the physical features of the River Einich and its valley from 917000 to 924046. **4** (KU)

(*b*) Explain how the waterfall in 9698 was likely to have been formed.

You may use diagram(s) to explain your answer. **3** (KU)

(*c*) Look at Reference Diagram Q1A and find area X on Reference Diagram Q1.

Using map evidence, suggest reasons why this area is suitable for commercial forestry. **4** (KU)

(*d*) What is the main present day function of Aviemore?

Choose from:

tourism and recreation *service centre*

Use map evidence to justify your choice. **5** (ES)

(*e*) A developer is proposing to build a wind farm of up to twenty wind turbines on Castle Hill in 9505 (see Reference Diagram Q1A).

Do you think this proposal should go ahead?

You must give map evidence to support your answer. **6** (ES)

Marks

KU	ES

1. (continued)

(*f*) **Reference Diagrams Q1F: Popular outdoor pursuits in the Aviemore area.**

This whole area is popular with hill walkers and skiers as illustrated in Reference Diagrams Q1F.

A group of school pupils want to gather information on the **impact** these groups have on the landscape.

Describe, in detail, the gathering techniques they might use.

Give reasons for your choice of techniques. 5

Marks

KU	ES

2. Reference Diagram Q2: Synoptic Chart for 6 am, 21st January 2010.

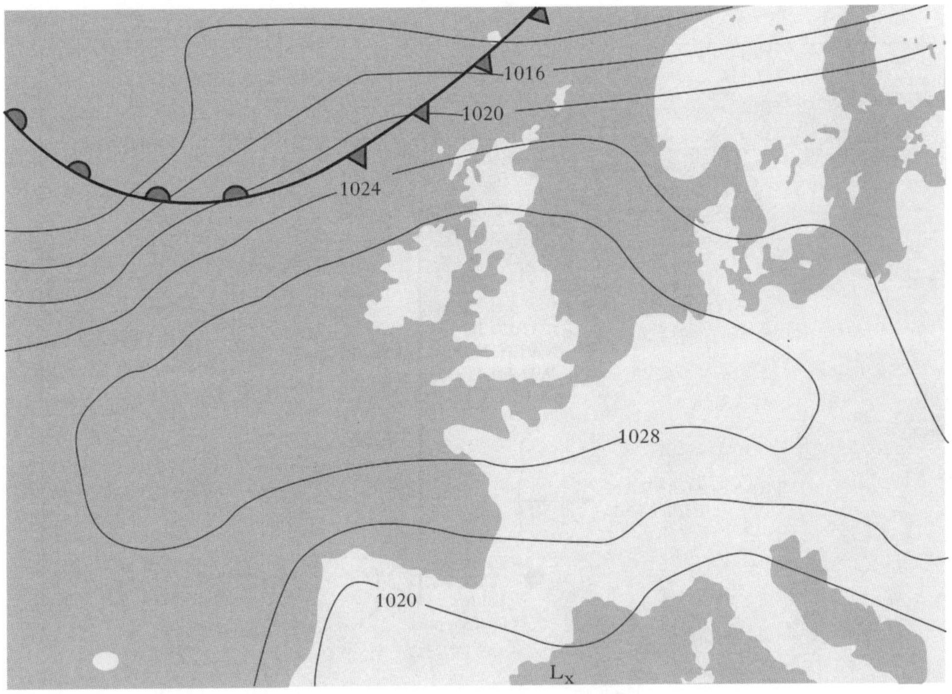

> *'In Scotland drivers should be careful of icy road conditions this morning and be aware that snow is likely during the evening rush hour.'*
>
> Statement by a weather forecaster

Explain fully why the weather forecaster announced this warning to motorists. **5**

Marks

KU	ES

3. Reference Diagram Q3: Trans-Alaskan pipeline facts.

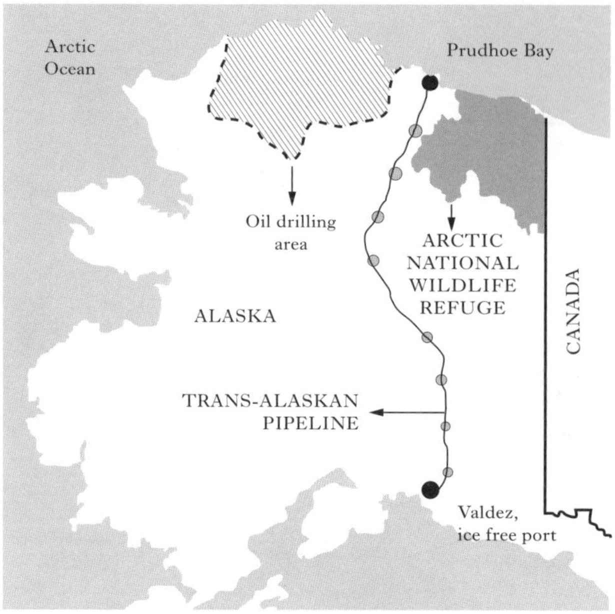

Recent burst pipe spilt 250,000 gallons of crude oil

Wildlife like reindeer migrate through the area

Drilling provides electricity and oil for locals

Thousands of tourists visit pipeline

Pipeline annually supplies 17% of USA's oil

Pipeline company employs over 2,000 workers

Pipeline runs near Copper River's salmon fisheries

The Trans-Alaskan pipeline has been pumping oil from the frozen north of Alaska to the ice-free port of Valdez for over thirty years. Even today there are many who argue that the extraction of the oil and the miles of pipeline should not have been allowed in such a fragile tundra environment.

Study Reference Diagram Q3.

"The oil industry in Alaska has brought only benefits to the local people and environment."

To what extent do you agree with this statement?

Give reasons for your answer.

Marks

KU	ES

4. Reference Diagram Q4: The Spheres of Influence of Three Shops in a city.

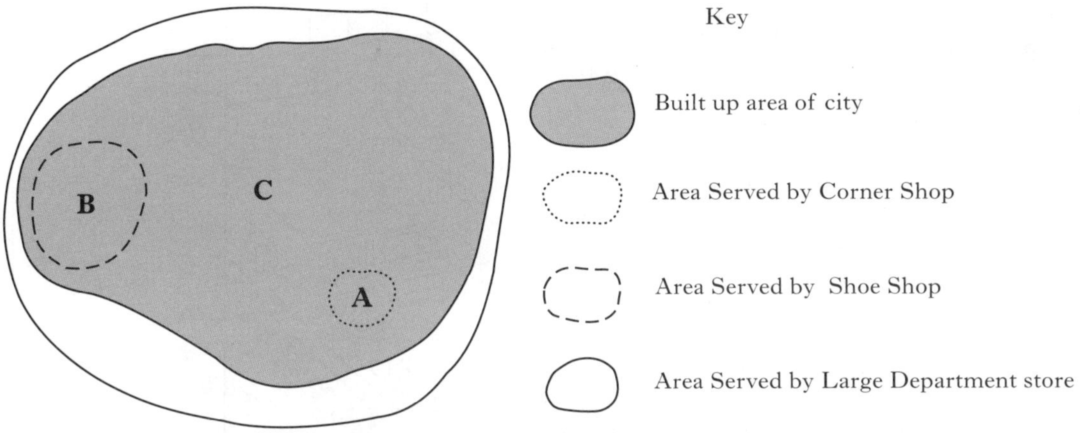

Look at Reference Diagram Q4.

Suggest reasons why the three shops have different sized spheres of influence. **4** (ES)

Marks KU ES

5. Reference diagram Q5A: A Modern Industrial Landscape.

Reference diagram Q5B: Industrial location factors for modern industry.

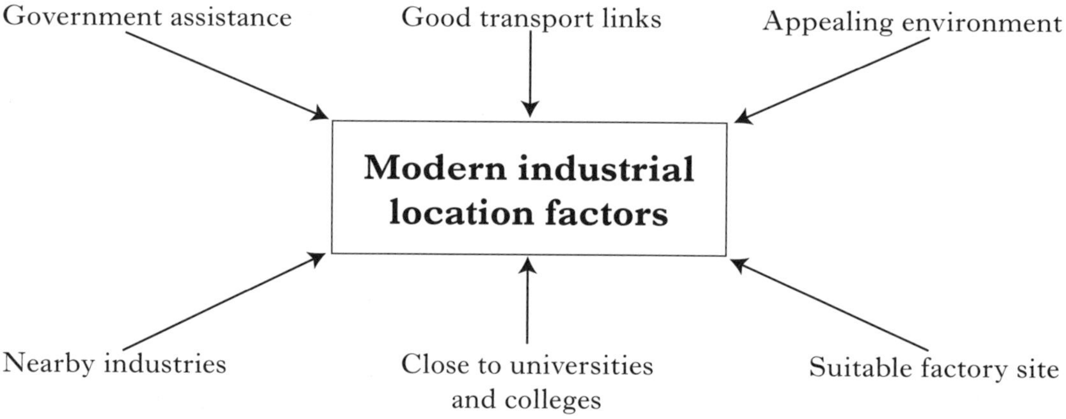

Study Reference Diagrams Q5A and Q5B.

Explain the ways in which the location factors listed above are important to modern industries. **6**

Marks KU ES

6. Reference Diagram Q6A: Two farms in Scotland.

Farm X

Farm Y

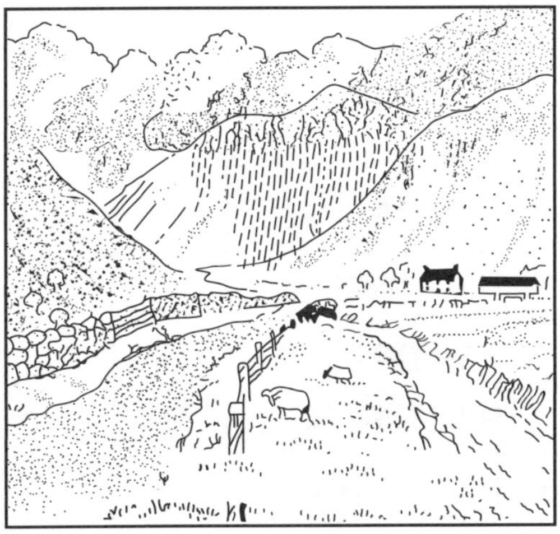

Reference Diagram Q6B – Selected Information on the Two Farms.

	Farm X	**Farm Y**
Number of farm workers	5 full time 12 part time	3 full time
Distance to nearest large town	16 km	48 km
Machinery	6 tractors 2 combine harvesters 10 other machines	2 tractors 7 other machines
Farm output (%)	35% Wheat 35% Barley 20% Potatoes 10% Strawberries	60% Lamb 20% Mutton 13% Wool 7% Turnips

(*a*) Study reference Diagrams Q6A and Q6B.

Give reasons for the differences shown between farms X and Y. **5**

(*b*) Describe other processing techniques which could be used to display the farm information shown in Reference Diagram Q6B. **5**

Marks KU ES

7. Reference Diagram Q7: Population Pyramids for Italy and Tanzania.

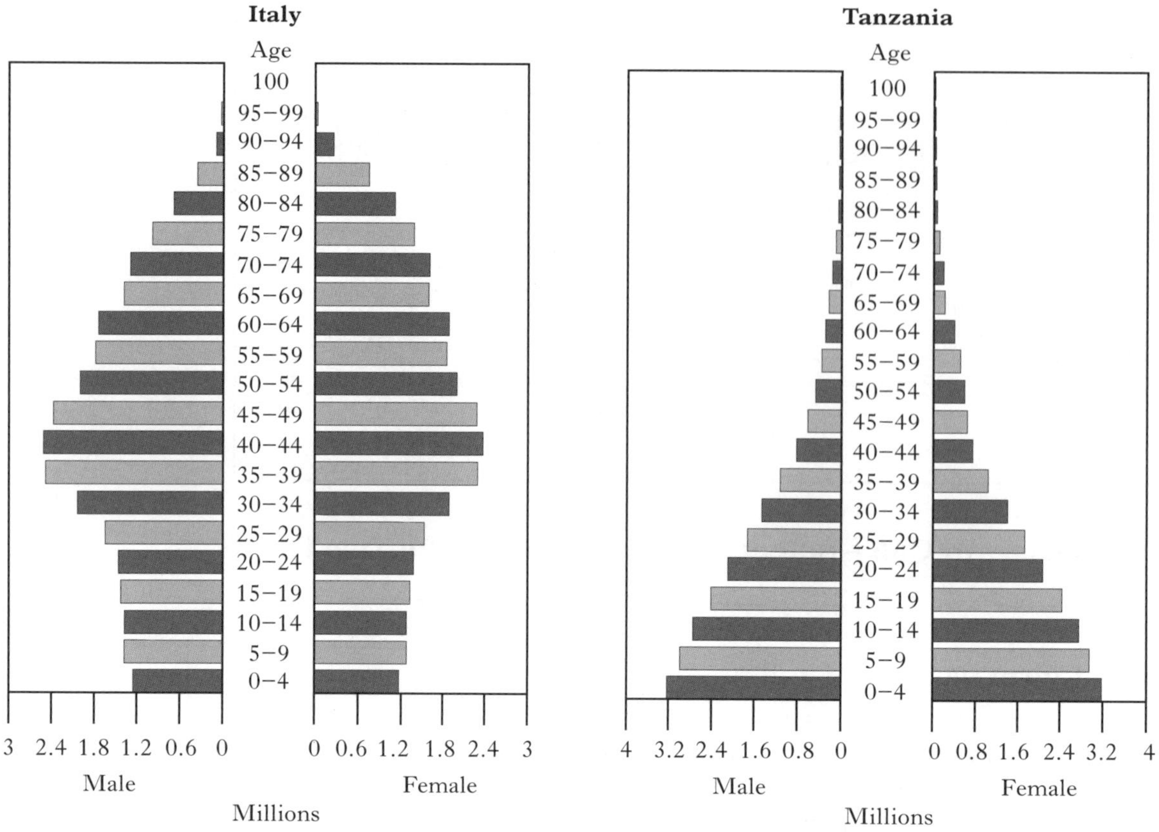

Study Reference Diagram Q7.

(*a*) Describe in detail the differences between the populations of Italy and Tanzania. ES 3

(*b*) Give reasons for the differences shown between the populations of Italy and Tanzania. KU 5

Marks

KU	ES

8. Reference Diagram Q8A: Malawi – Main Exports and Imports.

Exports	%	Imports	%
Foodstuffs	88	Manufactured goods	69
Fuels and mining products	1	Fuels and mining products	14
Manufactured goods	11	Foodstuffs	17
Total (£ million)	396	**Total (£ million)**	708

Reference Diagram Q8B: Malawi's Trading Partners.

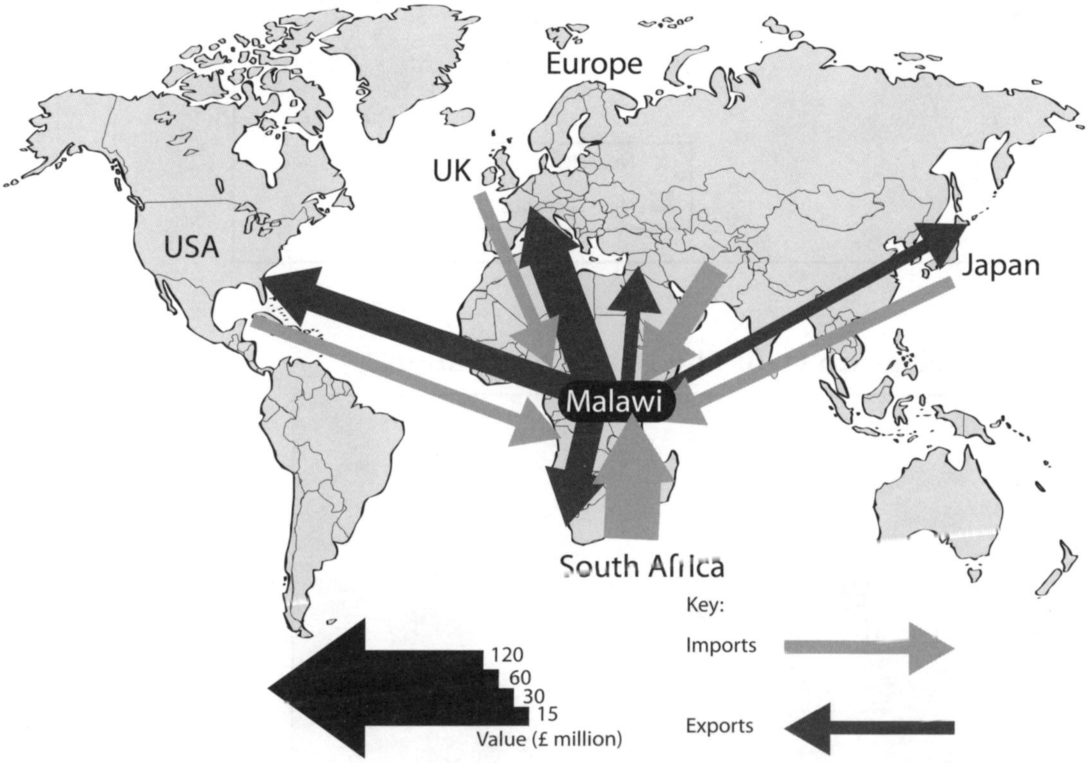

Export	Value (£ million)	Import	Value (£ million)
E.U.	55	South Africa	133
USA	25	Other African nations	48
South Africa	24	U.K.	17
Other African nations	16	Japan	13
Japan	11	U.S.A.	12

Study Reference Diagrams Q8A and Q8B.

Describe the pattern of Malawi's trade. **5**

Marks

KU	ES

9. Reference Diagram Q9A: Location of the Nike Corporation Worldwide.

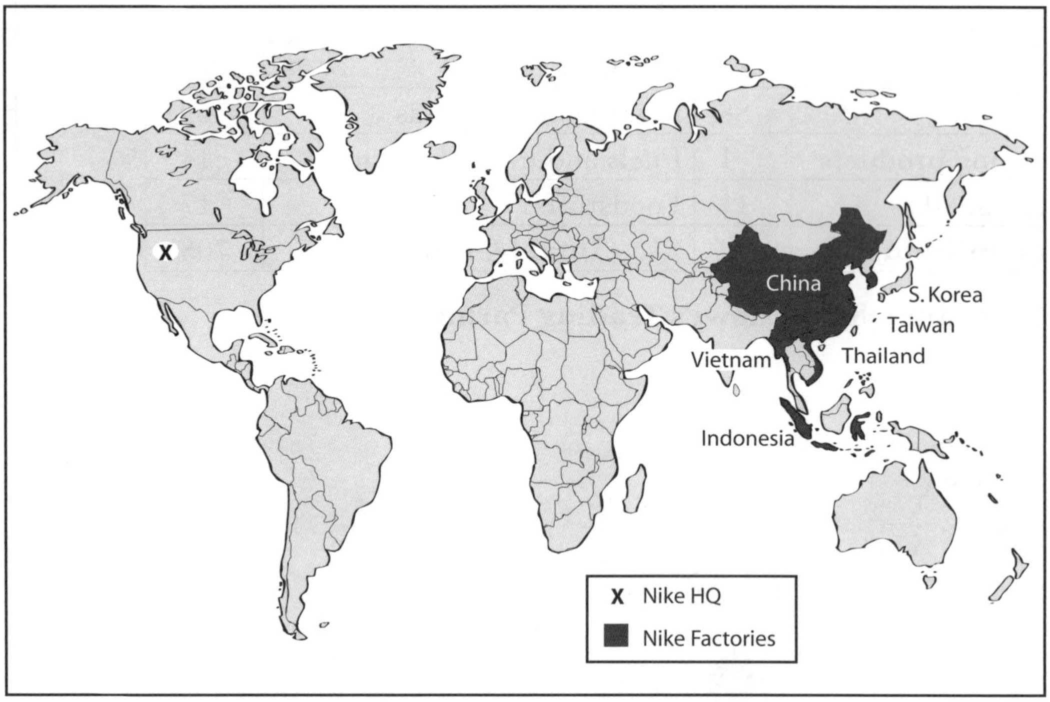

Reference Diagram Q9B: The Nike Corporation.

Nike Headquarters, Oregon, USA

Marks

KU	ES

9. (continued)

Reference Diagram Q9C: Nike factory, Vietnam.

Study Reference Diagrams Q9A, Q9B and Q9C.

Explain why most Multinational Corporations (MNCs) have their headquarters in a developed country and their factories in developing countries.

Give reasons for your answers. **5**

Marks

KU	ES

10. **Reference Diagram Q10A: Percentage of GDP spent by Developed Countries on Aid.**

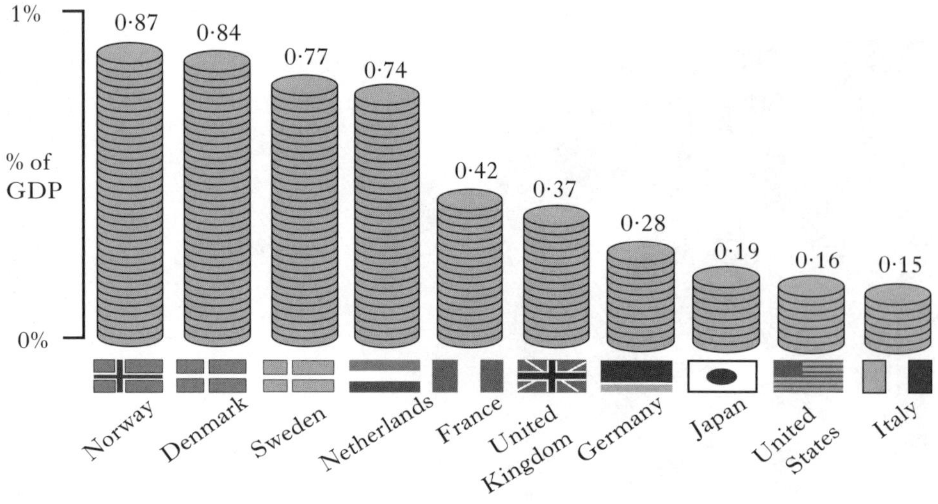

Reference Diagram Q10B: Possible reasons developed countries give aid to developing countries

- Orders increase in donor country
- Aid is often tied
- Forms political alliances
- Wider market to trade
- Developed countries can afford aid

Study reference Diagram Q10A and Q10B.

'Developed countries want to give aid to developing countries because of the benefits involved.'

Do you agree? Give reasons for your answer. **4**

Worked Answers

Guide to Worked Answers

Where applicable, a number of different answers have been provided to the practice questions to help you see the variety of answers available to choose from.

The number in brackets indicates how many marks the sentence is worth, e.g. (1) = 1 mark and (2) = 2 marks.

At the start of some answers, information on mark allocation is provided, e.g. 1 mark will be awarded for a correct point and 2 marks will be awarded for an extended point. This is to help you gauge how much information you need to write to obtain full marks. This is particularly important at credit level when you do not write on the specially set out question/answer paper.

When answering the mapwork question it is good practice to give a few grid references or named features because **marks can be awarded for correct grid references or named features, e.g. 'A45'.**

Some answers have specific information about how the question is marked – this will allow you to plan your answer carefully, e.g. at least **TWO** processing techniques must be given for full marks.

At the beginning of some answers you will see the following statement:

Marks can be awarded as follows: 1:3, 3:1 or 2:2.

This means that if a question asks for both advantages **and** disadvantages you can be awarded marks for a 4 mark question as follows:

1:3 means 1 mark for an advantage and 3 marks for disadvantages **OR**

3:1 means 3 marks for advantages and 1 mark for a disadvantage **OR**

2:2 means 2 marks for advantages and 2 for disadvantages.

PRACTICE EXAM A — GENERAL LEVEL WORKED ANSWERS

1. (*a*) The marks allocated for this type of answer are:

4 correct = 3 marks
3 or 2 correct = 2 marks
1 correct = 1 mark.

Physical Feature	**Grid Square**
Broad floodplain	3975
Gently sloping land	3784
Meander	3575
Tributaries meeting river	3775

3KU

HINT Look at the physical features that you know you can identify and leave the hardest physical features until last – you should be able to work through the answer by a process of elimination.

(*b*) 1 Mark will be awarded for each correct difference. Possible answers may include:

Earlsdon (3277) is an old 19th century housing area and Wood End (3682) is a newer 20th century housing area (1). Earlsdon is arranged in a grid-iron street pattern and Wood End is arranged in a modern street pattern with cul-de-sacs and crescents (1). This street pattern makes it safer for children as there will be no through-traffic (1). Earlsdon is closer to the Central Business District (CBD) so it will be more congested and have less open space (1) whereas in Wood End there is space for gardens and garages (1). Wood End is on the outskirts of Coventry (1). Houses in Earlsdon will be terraced and in Wood End they will be detached or semi-detached (1). In Wood End there are more open spaces/countryside and in Earlsdon there will be more pollution as it is built beside the CBD (1).
4KU

HINT Be careful not to describe other land uses as the question refers to differences between residential (housing) areas.

(*c*) 1 mark will be awarded for correct grid reference or named feature, e.g. 'A45'. Answers may include:

The business park has flat land to build on and expand (1). Room for a car park for workers (1). There are many settlements nearby such as Finham which will supply a workforce (1) and a market/customers (1). It is on the edge of the city of Coventry so the land will probably be cheap (1). The out-of-town location will provide a pleasant working environment (1). It is located right beside A45 (main road), so goods can be moved in and out easily/fast (1). The main road will also allow the workforce good access to their work (1). Coventry airport is right beside it so managers can fly in/out on business trips (1). Light raw materials/finished products can be flown in/out (1). Nearby motor works in grid square 3774 (1) may make component parts (1). The university in grid square 3478 (1) may provide a skilled work force for the business park (1) and/or keep the business park up-to-date with current research (1). **4ES**

HINT You must say 'flat land to expand' – you cannot just list flat land, road nearby, airport etc – develop each point that you make.

(*d*) Possible answers may include:

YES: Ryton-on-Dunsmore is close to Coventry (1). It is a separate village from Coventry city (1). It is located in the greenbelt (1). The main land use is residential (1). There are very few places of work (1) so many people would need to commute to get to their work (1). The A45 (main road) runs right through the settlement (1) and provides direct access into the CBD of Coventry (1).

NO: It has a post office, a pub and a church where people can work (1). The residents could also work in the nearby motor works (1). There is no direct train link between the two areas (1). Many young people prefer to live in the city nowadays and as it is located in the countryside, it may be occupied by mostly elderly people who no longer work (2). **4ES**

HINT You can answer either yes OR no to this question, as long as you give reasons for your choice.

(*e*) Marks for this question can be awarded as follows: 1:3, 3:1 or 2:2.

1 mark will be awarded for giving a correct grid reference or named feature, e.g. 'Lower Farm'.

1. (continued)

Answers may include:

FOR: There is forestry and small lakes which make the scenery pleasant/attractive (1). These features allow people to do various outdoor activities (1), e.g. orienteering in the woods (1) or water sports, such as canoeing, on the lakes (1). There is a visitor centre (1) and a nature reserve (1). Many people may visit as it is on the edge of the city (1). There is good access to this area with a railway and main roads nearby (1). There is room to build tourist facilities such as toilets (1). The hotel in grid square 3675 can be used by tourists who want to stay for a few days (1).

AGAINST: There is a motor works nearby which may cause noise and spoil the tranquillity (1). The main road and railway may also create noise pollution (1) and make it unsafe for small children (1). There are nearby farms, e.g. Lower Farm (1) and the people who come to visit may create problems for the farmer, such as dropping litter or leaving gates open (2). There is limited space to build a large car park (1). The river could flood tourist facilities such as the visitor centre (1). Or any other relevant point. **4ES**

HINT — Remember that a country park is an area of countryside where people go for leisure and recreational activities.

(*f*) An answer with well-labelled diagrams can obtain full marks.

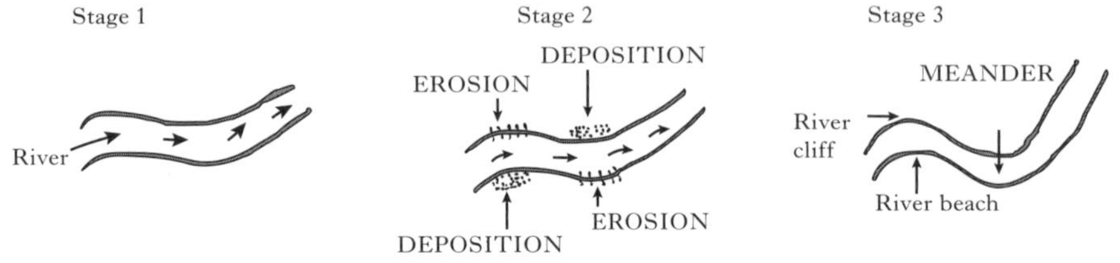

Answers may include:

A river rarely flows in a straight line – it will bend around something in its course, e.g. a tree or hard rock (1). The river contains areas of deep water and areas of shallow water (1); this causes its current to swing from side-to-side (1). The river flows faster on the outside and erodes the outside bends of a river channel (1) creating a river cliff (1). The river erodes by hydraulic action/solution/corrasion (1). The river flows more slowly on the inside bend of a river channel (1) creating a river beach/slip off slope (1). Over time these bends become more prominent, creating large meanders (1). **3KU**

HINT — These types of question want you to draw diagrams and space is provided on the exam paper for them.

2. An answer with well-labelled diagrams can obtain full marks.

Answers may include:

U-SHAPED VALLEY: During the ice-age snow collected and compressed to ice in a v-shaped river valley (1). Ice moved downhill under the force of gravity (1). Ice eroded the sides and bottom of the valley (1) using plucking (1); this is when the ice freezes onto rocks and, as it moves, the rocks are ripped from the mountain (1), and abrasion (1); this is when the rocks that are frozen in the base of the glacier wear away the bottom of the valley (1). The sides of the valley were made steeper and the bottom of the valley was widened (1), interlocking spurs were truncated (1). After the ice-age, when the ice had melted, a misfit stream or ribbon lake might have occupied the valley (1).

PYRAMIDAL PEAK: During the ice-age snow collected in hollows around a mountain (1). The snow turned to ice (1). Ice moved downhill under the force of gravity (1). The ice eroded the mountain on all sides (1) using plucking (1); this is when the ice freezes onto rocks and, as it moves, the rocks are ripped from the mountain (1), and abrasion (1); this is when the rocks that are frozen in the base of the glacier wear away the bottom of the hollows (1). This creates corries on all sides of the mountain (1). As the glaciers eroded backwards into the mountain, the corries got bigger (1); this produced a steep-sided peak between them (1). The peak was then weathered by frost shattering (1). **4KU**

The formation of a pyramidal peak

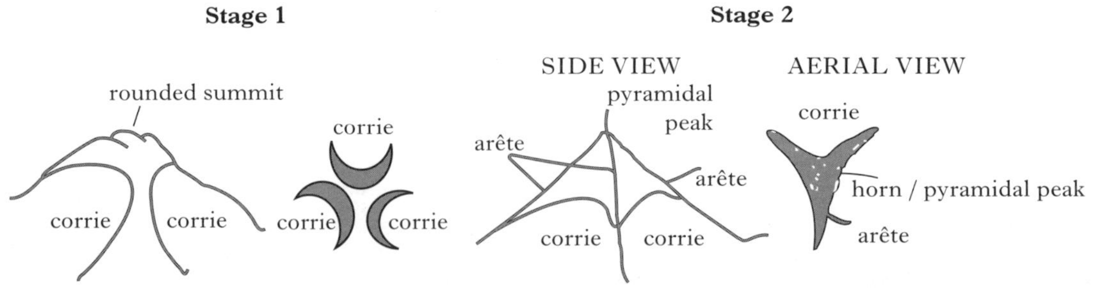

TOP EXAM TIP

Always ensure that your diagrams are fully labelled and explained.

3. Answers may include:

EAST: Light cloud with sunny intervals (1). Temperatures between 4°C and 5°C (1). Dry (1).

WEST: Thick cloud with rain showers (1). Temperatures between 6°C and 7°C (1).

East warmer than west (1). West wetter than east (1). West cloudier than east (1). **4ES**

HINT Make sure you know your west from your east – remember the compass reads across the word 'WE'.

4. (*a*) Correct answer: **2KU**

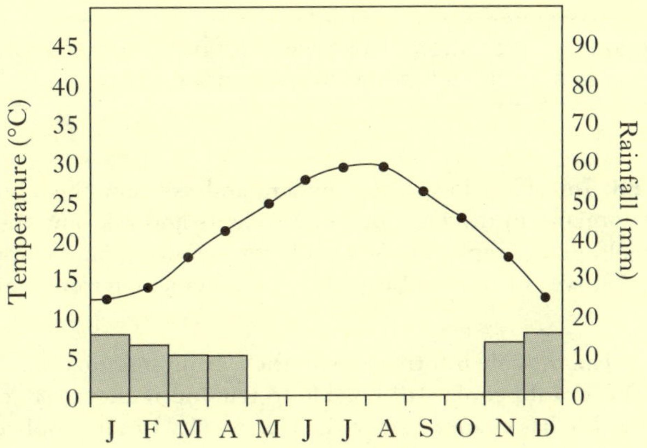

HINT Remember rainfall figures are shown by bars on a climate graph.

(*b*) Answers may include: Highest temperature is 29°C and it occurred in July and August (1) Lowest temperature is 13°C and it occurred in December and January (1) Average temperature is 22°C (1) Range in temperature is 16°C (1) Highest rainfall is 15 mm and it occurred in January and December (1) Lowest rainfall is 0 mm and it occurred in May to October (1) Total annual rainfall is 74 mm (1) Average rainfall is 6 mm (1) The relationship between temperature and rainfall is the higher the temperature, the lower the rainfall (1) This is a hot desert climate (1). **4ES**

TOP EXAM TIP

You must mention both temperature AND rainfall with months for full marks.

5. 1 mark will be awarded for a correct point and 2 marks will be awarded for an extended point. Answers may include:

AGREE: New roads have made it easier to move around (1). This brings in new companies to the rainforest, e.g. commercial farming and mining (1). Local people can get jobs and earn money in the new industries (1). Hydro-electric power stations provide cheap electricity for the people (1). Land has been cleared for cattle ranching, increasing the food supply (1). Developments can provide the country with more money from trading goods (1) and this money can be used to help develop the country and improve the standard of living of the local people (1).

DISAGREE: Areas of rainforest have been cleared to make space for new developments, reducing the area and number of trees that provide local people with their food (1). Large areas of land have been flooded for hydro-electric power plants – reducing the area that local people can live off (1). Rivers are polluted from waste from the mines (1). Local people have been forced to leave their homes (1). There is increased soil erosion as the protective canopy has been removed (1) so fewer crops can be grown (1). New developments have attracted outsiders who have brought diseases that natives have no immunity to (1). Local peoples' traditional way of live is disappearing as they are employed in new industries (1). New roads bring cars which pollute the landscape (1). Fewer trees means more carbon dioxide in the atmosphere (1) and potentially an increase in global warming (1). **4ES**

HINT Be careful <u>not</u> to list the changes in one sentence, e.g. logging, new roads, cattle ranching, mining, HEP.

6. (*a*) 1 mark will be awarded for a simple point and 2 marks will be awarded for an expanded point. Answers may include:

SOCIAL: Unemployment/loss of jobs (1). This will lead to a greater strain on social services (1). Social security payments will increase (1). There may be an increase in crime rates in the area (1).

ECONOMIC: Local shops may close due to locals having less money to spend (1). House prices will fall as people leave the area to look for work (1). Small local businesses that relied on the factory and provided services to it, may also close down (1).

ENVIRONMENTAL: The derelict factory will look unsightly if left abandoned (1). Whole area becomes run-down (1) due to derelict factory, vandalism, graffiti etc (1). The quality of the air may improve due to less delivery lorries in the area (1). **4KU**

HINT You don't need to separate your answer into social, economic and environmental effects BUT you do have to include aspects of them all in your answer.

(*b*) Answers. may include:

GATHERING TECHNIQUES: Interview local shop owners and ask how their business has been affected (1). Send out a questionnaire to the local people/residents and ask how the factory closure has affected them (1). Obtain old photographs of the area from the library and compare with recent photographs (1). Do a land use survey of the landscape (1). Conduct an environmental quality index survey of the area (1).

REASONS: Local shop owners can provide information on their profit margins (1). This information is first-hand and up-to-date (1). Local people will be able to tell you if they were employed by the factory and how their quality of life has changed since the closure (1). Local people can comment on the decline of services in the area as they live there (1); they can comment on the changes/appearance of the landscape, e.g. graffiti (1). Analysing old and new photographs will give you a visual comparison of the changes in the area (1). Photographs can be annotated to highlight the changes (1). A land use survey will provide up-to-date information that can be compared with maps from the past (1). An environmental quality index survey will allow you to determine the quality of the environment (1); or any other relevant point. **4ES**

TOP EXAM TIP

You MUST state who you will interview or what type of map you will use – you cannot just write down interview, survey, maps as this is not specific enough.

7. Marks for this question can be awarded as follows: 1:3, 3:1 or 2:2.

Answers may include:

ADVANTAGES: Bigger field sizes allow machinery to be used (1) making work quicker and easier for the farmer (1). Removing hedges provides more farm land so higher yields can be achieved/more crops can be grown (1); this increases the farmer's profits (1). Fewer farm workers means less wages to be paid (1). The use of fertilisers and pesticides improves crop yields (1). Larger farms allow the farmer to achieve economies of scale (1).

DISADVANTAGES: Removing hedges destroys animals' habitats (1). Less farm workers increase unemployment in rural areas (1); this can force people to leave the countryside in search of work (1). As a result of the declining population, the number of rural services decline (1). Fertilisers and pesticides pollute nearby rivers (1). Or any other relevant point. **4ES**

HINT DO NOT lift straight from the source – <u>use</u> the information in the diagrams to help you write an answer.

8. Answers may include:

YES: Cities in developing countries are more likely to have more health services, e.g. hospitals (1). Improved access to education facilities such as schools and universities (1). Better job opportunities in different industries (1). Higher wages (1). Access to more entertainment facilities (1). Better housing (1). Reliable food supply (1). Better standard of living (1).

NO: Cities in developing countries are more likely to have higher crime rates (1). Many houses are in shanty towns (1) which lack basic services like piped water and sanitation (1). This can lead to diseases such as typhoid and cholera which can kill people (1). There is high unemployment due to over-population (1). People are separated from their extended families in the countryside (1) and they are disillusioned that their expectations of a better life in the city are not fulfilled (1). **4KU**

HINT You can include points on yes AND no since the question refers to both rural and urban areas.

9. (*a*) Answers may include: The UK has fewer people in the young age groups from 0–10 (1). There are approximately 14 million young dependents, i.e. 0–15 (1). The UK has a low infant mortality rate (1) and a high life expectancy (1); this is shown by the bullet shape (1). The UK also has a low death rate (1). There are approximately 11 million people aged 65+ in the UK (1). **3ES**

> *HINT* — Describe in detail means that you have to quote figures from the source provided.

(*b*) There will be fewer children born so some schools and nurseries may have to close (1). As a result of this, some teachers may lose their jobs (1). The Government will need to spend more money and invest in resources for the elderly and spend less money on education (2). The Government will also need to invest more money in care homes, pensions and bus passes for the growing elderly population (2). There will be fewer people in the working age group (1); as a result there may be a shortage of workers (1). There will also be a shortage of skilled labour (1). The Government may have to spend money attracting foreign workers to fill certain job vacancies (1). **4KU**

> *HINT* — Try to give relevant examples to improve the overall quality of your answer.

10. At least **TWO** processing techniques must be given for full marks. Marks can be awarded as follows: 1:3, 3:1 or 2:2. Answers may include:

PROCESSING TECHNIQUES:	**REASON(S):**
Multiple bar graph (1)	Different colours can be used to show the differences between the imports and exports (1).
Pie charts (1)	The numbers are already in percentages (1). Drawing 2 pie charts – 1 for imports and the other for exports – will allow easy comparisons to be made (1).
Divided bar graphs (1)	The figures are already in percentages so there is no need to spend time converting them (1). Placing 2 divided bar graphs side by side/one above the other will make it easy to compare the imports and exports (1).
Pictograms (1)	A series of pictures for both imports and exports would be needed (1). The illustrations may be easier to interpret without having to look at a key (which you would have to do for the pie charts and bar graphs) (1). **4ES**

> *HINT* — The same reason cannot be awarded more than 1 mark – even if it is given for a different technique.

11. 1 mark will be awarded for a correct point and 2 marks will be awarded for an extended point. Answers may include:

SHORT-TERM AID: Emergency food supplies will help to feed the people who have lost everything (1) and prevent starvation (1). Clean water will stop people dying from dehydration (1) and limit the spread of disease (1). Medical supplies can be used to treat people with injuries (1) and stop infections and/or disease spreading (1). Rescue workers will help to find trapped people (1). Blankets and tents will provide people with shelter (1).

LONG-TERM AID: Houses would need to be rebuilt to help people rebuild their lives (1). Businesses would have to be rebuilt to help get the country's economy going again (1). Schools would need to be rebuilt to provide education (1). Water supplies and sanitation pipes would need to be properly re-connected (1) to prevent further spread of disease (1). Electricity cables would have to be safely restored (1). Bridges and communications would need to be rebuilt (1). Farming equipment would have to be replaced in order to secure food supplies (1) and ensure self-sufficiency of future food supplies (1). **3ES**

> *HINT* — You must only give reasons <u>for the choice</u> you have ticked.

PRACTICE EXAM A — CREDIT LEVEL WORKED ANSWERS

1. (*a*) (i) The marks allocated for this type of answer are:

4 correct = 3 marks
3 or 2 correct = 2 marks
1 correct = 1 mark.

Glacial Feature	**Grid Reference**
U-shaped valley with ribbon lake	725106
Corrie	710115
Pyramidal peak	709129
Arête	719119

3KU

HINT: Use a pencil to circle the grid references on your map – this will help you to compare the features. Clue: a pyramidal peak will usually have a spot height.

(ii) An answer with well-labelled diagrams can obtain full marks.
Answers may include:

The formation of a corrie.

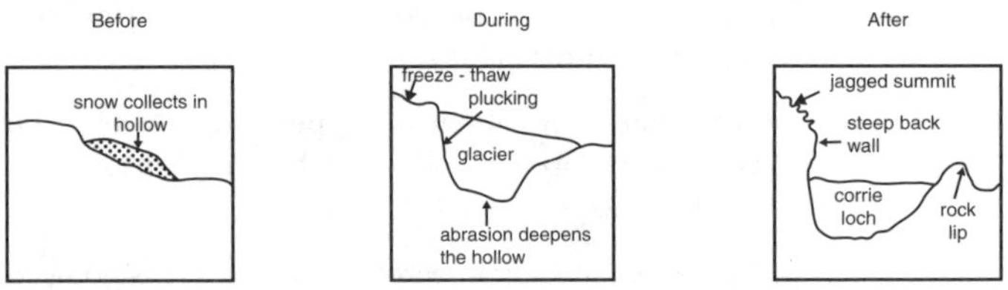

CORRIE: During the ice-age snow gathered in a colder, north facing hollow (1). As the snow piled up, the bottom layers were compressed by the weight into ice (1). The ice began to move downhill under the force of gravity (1). The ice eroded the hollow by plucking and abrasion (1). The rotational movement of the ice helped to create a deep hollow (1) and a rock lip was formed by over-deepening (1). When the ice eventually melted, a steep back wall had been created and the hollow was much deeper (1). **4KU**

TOP EXAM TIP

It is essential that the main features on your diagrams are correctly <u>labelled</u>.

(*b*) Answers may include:

Steep slopes will create fast flowing water (1). The river upstream from the waterfall can be dammed to create a reservoir (1). Impermeable rock would allow water to be stored (1). This is a high land area so there will be plenty of rainfall (1) also indicated by many streams (1). Difference in land height will allow the water to fall from a high level to drive the turbines built at a lower level (1). The difficult terrain (steep slopes) means that the area is unsuitable for building on (1). The reservoir will provide water to nearby settlements (1). The HEP will provide the area with an alternative form of energy (1) that is more environmentally friendly (1). The settlements nearby would provide a labour force to build the power station (1) and also to run and maintain it (1). The main road (A493) will provide access for workers to the power station (1). **4KU**

HINT: Use the information in the grid reference given first AND then look at the rest of the map to help you answer this question.

(*c*) Marks for this question can be awarded as follows: 3:3, 4:2 or 2:4.

1 mark awarded for correct grid reference or named feature, e.g. 'Panorama Walk'. Maximum of 2 marks for a list of activities.

Answers may include:

ADVANTAGES: There is a beach, forestry and hills which make the scenery attractive (1). This allows people to do various outdoor activities (1), e.g. orienteering in the woods, hill walking, sight-seeing, or water sports such as canoeing on the blue lake or jet-skiing in the sea, or picnics by the waterfalls (2). There is a leisure centre (1), a nature reserve (1) (723125) (1) and various walks/trails (1). The coastal location of Barmouth allows for sunbathing in summertime (1). The outdoor pursuit centre will provide instruction/lessons in outdoor activities (1). There is good access to this area with a ferry port, railway and main roads (A496) (2). There are tourist facilities such as toilets and car parking facilities (1) (639148) (1). There are hotels that can be used by tourists who want to stay for a few days (1). There is a tourist information centre that can provide information on activities/places to eat/visit etc (1).

1. (continued)

DISADVANTAGES: Steep land may be inaccessible/difficult for very old or very young people (1). Tourists may get lost in the remote hills and there are very few public telephones/places to get help (2). The main road and railway may create noise pollution and spoil the tranquillity of the area (2) and make it unsafe for small children (1). The commercial forestry may spoil some of the scenery (1). There are many tourist facilities which may spoil the natural look of the area (1) for example, caravan sites. Barmouth is a port and may get very busy during peak season (1). Or any other relevant point.

6ES

HINT — You must give advantages <u>AND</u> disadvantages to obtain full marks for this question.

(*d*) Marks for this question can be awarded as follows: 3:2 or 2:3.

Answers may include:

GATHERING TECHNIQUES: Interview local shop owners and ask how their business has been affected by an increase in tourism (1). Send out a questionnaire to the local people/residents and ask how the tourists have affected them (1). Obtain old photographs of the area from the library and compare with recent photographs (1). Do a land use survey of the landscape (1). Conduct an environmental quality index survey of the area (1). Conduct a traffic survey during peak season (summer) and compare with an off-peak (winter) traffic survey (1).

REASONS: Local shop owners can provide information on their profit margins (1). This information is first-hand and up-to-date (1). Local people will be able to tell you if they are affected by tourists and how their quality of life has changed since the increase in tourism (1). Local people can comment on the increase in services in the area as they live there (1). They can comment on the changes/appearance of the landscape, e.g. litter/tourist facilities (1). Analysing old and new photographs will give you a visual comparison of the changes in the area (1). Photographs can be annotated to highlight the key features (1). A land use survey will provide up-to-date information that can be compared with maps from the past (1). This will highlight the increase in tourist facilities (1). An environmental quality index survey will allow you to determine the quality of the environment (1); or any other relevant answer.

5ES

HINT — You MUST give detailed descriptions of the gathering techniques that you would use – imagine that you had to go out and do the fieldwork for yourself.

(*e*) 1 mark will be awarded for a simple point and 2 marks will be awarded for an expanded point. 1 mark awarded for a named example, e.g. Fairbourne nature centre.

Answers may include:

Conflict between locals and tourists: tourist traffic congests roads and impedes local people from going about their everyday business (1), especially on narrow coastal roads (1). Tourists parking on narrow coastal road or in inappropriate areas may also conflict with local people (1). Conflict between conservation aims of a National Park area and developers who want to build more houses, e.g. in Fairbourne or extend tourist facilities (2). Conflicts between conservationists and hill walkers who erode footpaths and drop litter spoiling the look of the area (2). Conflict between farmers and tourists: tourists object to farmers restricting access to their land (1), tourists can damage farm fences/walls (1), tourists leave gates open and drop litter (1) which can put the animals in danger (1), tourists' dogs can worry sheep (1). Conflict between golfers and walkers over access to different areas (1). Conflict between conservationists and the forestry commission: the forestry companies want to plant trees and conservationists do not want rows of trees spoiling the natural scenery/blocking views (1). Conflict between conservationists and tourists over damage caused to historical places of interest (1) such as standing stones (1) and who cause water pollution by dropping litter (1) or by using jet-skis (1). Railway may disturb residents in houses or tourists staying at the hotel (1). Or any other relevant point.

4ES

HINT — Remember that a conflict is a <u>disagreement</u> between two different land users/groups of people.

2. (*a*) Answer: temperature is 8°C (1). 2 oktas of cloud cover (1). SW wind direction (1). 15 knots wind speed (1). Dry (1).

4KU

HINT — This part of the question requires you to describe, i.e. say what the weather station symbol shows.

2. (continued)

(*b*) 1 mark will be awarded for a simple point and 2 marks will be awarded for an expanded point.

Answers may include: Air pressure will fall as the warm front approaches Edinburgh (1). Cloud cover will increase because a front is simply a band of cloud (1). Steady rain will fall because fronts bring rain (1). Wind speed will increase as indicated by the isobars being closer together (1). As the warm front moves away, Edinburgh will be in the warm sector of a depression (1). Temperatures will increase slightly and it will be mild (1). There may be a few clouds which may bring a few showers (1). As the cold front appears over Edinburgh, cloud cover will increase and heavy rain will fall (2). Temperatures will drop as the cold front passes and leaves Edinburgh in the cold sector (1). The sky will become clear (1), rainfall will stop (1) and air pressure will increase (1). Wind speeds will decrease (1) and the weather will visibly improve as the low pressure system moves away from Edinburgh (1). **6KU**

HINT

This part of the question requires you to give reasons for the type of weather described in part (a). At credit level you must be able to talk about the weather associated with fronts and depressions.

3. Marks for this question can be awarded as follows: 3:3, 4:2 or 2:4.

Answers may include:

FOR: Many jobs will be created lowering unemployment (1); this is particularly important in times of recession (1). Much energy will be generated from the UK's wind-swept coastline (1). The shallow waters will allow the turbines to be constructed (1). The money generated will boost the whole of the UK's economy (1) enabling money to be invested into services, e.g. schools, hospitals etc (1) and perhaps other schemes for more renewable sources of energy (1). There will be a reduction in pollution from coal and oil-fired power stations (1). Increased use of renewable energy (1) will help to conserve finite resources (1). Wind turbines will be built off-shore so few people will see them (1). The UK will become more self-sufficient in power supplies (1).

AGAINST: The natural beauty of the coastline will be spoilt by many turbines (1). Wind turbines are very expensive to build (1). Building and maintenance will be very difficult as they are located in the sea (1). Some water pollution will occur in the building and maintenance of the turbines (1). Wind turbines are weather dependent so if there is no wind, no power will be generated (1). They may have to have alternative sources of energy for calm weather (1). The turbines could be a danger to ships at sea (1) and birds may fly into them and get injured or die (1). Or any other relevant point. **6ES**

TOP EXAM TIP

'To what extent' means that you should give arguments for AND against the given statement. You must use the source BUT do not lift information straight from it.

4. 1 mark will be awarded for a simple point and 2 marks will be awarded for an expanded point. A maximum of 1 mark is awarded for description only. To obtain full marks, you must refer to both areas. Answers may include:

INNER CITY: Tenement flats/terraced housing was built to save space (1) **as** this area is beside the city centre where the cost of land is most expensive (1); this allowed a high density of housing to be concentrated in a small area (1). Housing in the inner city was built beside factories **because** people had to walk to work (1) **as** cars had not yet been invented (1). There is a lack of gardens and open space **as** land was limited (1).

SUBURBAN AREAS: Detached/semi-detached housing is built on the edge of the city **as** there is more space beside the greenbelt (1). There is a lower housing density **because** the land is cheaper on the outskirts (1). This area has newer housing that was planned so there is a curvilinear street pattern with cul-de-sacs and crescents (1). Houses are larger with gardens and garages **as** there is more land and open space (1). **6KU**

HINT

When answering an explain question, you should always use the words 'because' or 'as'.

5. Marks for this question can be awarded as follows: 3:2 or 2:3.

Answers may include:

SET-ASIDE LAND

BENEFITS: Farmers are paid by the EU not to grow crops in certain field(s) (1). This means that they are getting money at no cost to themselves (1). Set-aside may pay better than the crops in the fields (1). Farmers are allowed to use the set-aside field(s) for diversification (1), e.g. camp site or quad-biking (1), increasing their income (1).

PROBLEMS: Farmers have to apply to the Government for the money on an annual basis (1) and the forms are complicated and lengthy to complete (1). Farmers may not be able to generate economies of scale without putting all their fields into crop production (1).

5. (continued)

ORGANIC FARMING

BENEFITS: Higher prices are available for crops that are produced without chemical fertilisers (1). The farmer can meet the demands of supplying organic produce to different suppliers (1) and he/she is able to become a responsible steward of the countryside by NOT using harmful chemicals (1).

PROBLEMS: Organic crops are much more costly to produce (1) and therefore cost more to buy (1) so farmers may find it difficult to compete with non-organic farmers (1). Chemical fertilisers help to produce more crops (1) and increase the farmer's profits but this option is not available to an organic farmer (1).

SUBSIDIES

BENEFITS: Farmers are given money by the EU to help support their farm (1). This helps to increase the farmer's standard of living (1) and helps them continue farming instead of going out of business (1). This is important as many farmers manage the land in the countryside (1).

PROBLEMS: Many Scottish hill farms would not be viable without the subsidies (1) so if the money was cut, some farmers might go out of business (1). Scottish farmers face competition for subsidies from other farmers in the EU (1) as The Common Agricultural Policy helps many European farmers (1).

DIVERSIFICATION

BENEFITS: This means that farmers are less reliant on producing only food to generate an income (1) and are therefore more financially secure (1). It allows the farmer to develop other skills (1) and means that the farmer can help educate people in rural life as he/she may open up a petting farm (1) or sell his/her produce in a farm shop (1). People have more leisure time nowadays and are likely to go and spend money on different activities (1).

PROBLEMS: It may be difficult to obtain planning permission to convert old barns into holiday cottages (1). Some people who come to visit the farm may drop litter (1) or leave gates open allowing animals to stray into danger (1) or their dogs may worry the sheep (1). The farm may be remote and it would be difficult to attract a high number of visitors (1). **5ES**

HINT: Underline you choice and other key words in your answer – this will help you to see the points that you have made more clearly.

6. Answers may include:

The factory has flat land to build on/expand (1). Room for a car park for workers (1). There are many settlements nearby such as Cumbernauld which will supply a workforce (1) and a market/customers (1). It is on the edge of the city of Glasgow so the land will probably be cheap (1). Out-of-town location will provide a pleasant working environment (1). Right beside A80, so goods can be imported/exported easily/fast (1). Main road will also allow the workforce good access to their work (1). Nearby industries may share ideas/resources/transport costs (1). Or any other relevant point. **5ES**

HINT: Explain each point that you make **in detail.** You should write at least one sentence per mark.

7. 1 mark will be awarded for a simple point and 2 marks will be awarded for an expanded point. Answers may include:

Population is unevenly distributed throughout Brazil due to a number of physical and human factors (1). Some areas such as the SE and major towns and cities, e.g. Sao Paulo are densely populated (2). Other areas, such as the Amazon Rainforest in the north of the country, are sparsely populated (1) because the climate is too inhospitable (1) and there is a lack of communications and industry (2). Some parts of the coastline are very crowded (1). Areas with high rainfall are sparsely populated because it is too difficult to farm the land (1). Areas with high land/mountains are sparsely populated because it is too cold to live there (1). Also, steep slopes are difficult to build on (1) and mountainous areas are often remote and difficult to get to (1). Soil quality tends to be poor and crops cannot be grown in mountainous regions (1). Areas where there is a lot of industry are crowded because people will go there to look for work (1). Or any other relevant point. **4ES**

HINT: Be careful: do not just describe what the maps are showing. You MUST give reasons for the population distribution.

8. (*a*) Answers may include:

India is at stage 3 of the Demographic Transition Model (1). It has high (1) but falling birth rates (1) and low death rates (1). This means that the overall population is growing rapidly (1).

4ES

HINT: This is an enquiry skills question – use the information in the diagrams to get full marks for this answer.

8. (continued)

(*b*) Answers may include:

Countries such as India are reducing their birth rates by establishing family planning clinics (1) and promoting the use of contraception (1). Vaccination programmes improve children's health and reduce infant mortality rates, (1) both of which encourage couples to have fewer children (1). Improved education for women means they become more aware of the importance of safe and clean drinking water (1) reducing infant mortality (1). Improved education also gives women more opportunities to work and this increases the likelihood that they will have fewer children (1). Some Governments provide financial incentives for families who have fewer children (1) or pass laws that penalise couples for having many children (1), e.g. China's one child policy (1). Or any other relevant point. **5KU**

HINT Write at least one sentence per mark to ensure you write enough detail in your answer.

9. (*a*) You will get 1 mark for a direct description of the graphs. 1 mark will be given for each valid difference between the graphs and 2 marks will be awarded for an extended point. Answers may include: the USA imports more industrial supplies than it exports (1). The USA imports 32% consumer goods and exports just under half this figure (1). It imports 5% agricultural products and exports 9% (1). The USA doesn't appear to import or export any raw materials (1). It imports 30% capital goods and almost half its total exports are capital goods – 49% (1), e.g. computers and office machines (1). **4ES**

HINT This question asks you to describe – say what you see and quote some figures.

(*b*) At least **TWO** processing techniques must be given for full marks. Marks can be awarded as follows: 2:3 or 3:2. You will be awarded a maximum of 3 marks only if no reasons are given or if you only state 1 technique. Answers may include:

PROCESSING TECHNIQUES:	**REASON(S):**
Bar graphs (1)	Drawing 2 bar graphs – 1 for imports and the other for exports – will allow easy comparisons to be made (1). Different colours can be used to show the differences between the imports and exports (1).
Pie charts (1)	The numbers are already in percentages (1). Drawing 2 pie charts – 1 for imports and the other for exports – will allow easy comparisons to be made (1). Colour can be used to highlight the different segments (1).
Table (1)	A table could be drawn with the imports in one column and exports in the other (1). Both imports and exports could be placed in order, with the most popular import and export at the top (1).
Pictograms (1)	A series of pictures for both imports and exports would be needed (1). The illustrations may be easier to interpret without having to look at a key (like you would have to do for the pie charts and bar graphs) (1).

5ES

HINT You must give **different** reasons for each technique.

PRACTICE EXAM B GENERAL LEVEL WORKED ANSWERS

1. (*a*) The marks allocated for this type of question are:

4 correct = 3 marks
3 or 2 correct = 2 marks
1 correct = 1 mark.

Feature on map	Letter
Outskirts of Addingham	B
Primary road	A
Forestry	D
River	C

3KU

HINT Work your way along the transect looking for the most obvious features like buildings, roads and rivers. Remember you have been given a key for your map so if you are not sure what colour a primary road is – look it up! You should be able to work through the answer by a process of elimination.

(*b*) An answer with well-labelled diagrams can obtain full marks.

Answers may include:

Erosion occurs on the outside bend where the river flows fastest (1) and deposition occurs on inside bend where water slows down (1). This causes the neck of the meander to narrow (1). During a storm or flood the river will break through the neck creating a new, straighter, channel (1). Deposition cuts off the old meander to form an ox-bow lake (1).

[Note: you will not get a mark for simply mentioning a meander, you must explain the formation process in detail.] **4KU**

HINT Best answers will outline the development of an ox-bow lake in a logical order using well-labelled diagrams to illustrate each stage.

(*c*) Marks for this question can be awarded as follows: 1:3, 2:2 or 3:1.

Possible gathering techniques: Measure width of river using a measuring tape (1). Measure depth of river using a measuring pole (1). Measure speed of river by timing a float passing through a measured distance (1) or with a flowmeter (1). Use an Ordnance Survey map (1). Take a photograph (1) or draw a field sketch of the river (1).

Possible justifications: Measurements can be compared with others taken at different times or at different places on the river's course (1). Use a measuring pole to help find if the channel in the river was shallow on the inner bend and deeper on the outside (1). Photographs can be compared with older pictures of the same part of the river (1). Field sketches can be annotated to highlight major points (1). OS map can show height of land and any river features (1).

Or any other relevant point. **4ES**

TOP EXAM TIP

For a gathering technique you must relate your answer to the actual question being asked, i.e. if you say you would take a photograph you must say what it is that you are actually photographing and be able to state why this photograph would be a good way of collecting information about a river.

(*d*) Answers may include:

Yes: surrounded by steep slopes for rock climbing, abseiling (1), river available for water activities, e.g. raft building, canoeing (1), forest trails through Middleton Woods for walking or orienteering (1). Pupils could visit the museum in 115478 (1), nearby Ilkley could be visited in pupils' free time or for shops (1). The A65 provides good access to the centre (1).

No: Centre is in quite an isolated area (1), only one main road into the area (1), there may be very little for the pupils to do in poor weather (1).

Or any other relevant point. **4ES**

HINT Think! – How could the pupils get there and what activities could they do once they were there?

1. (continued)

(*e*) Marks for this question can be awarded as follows: 1:3, 2:2 or 3:1.

You will be awarded a maximum of 1 mark for giving a correct grid reference.

Answers may include:

ADVANTAGES: Most of the route is through open, pleasant countryside (1).The footpath passes interesting historic features (1), e.g. enclosure 136448, pancake stone (1). There are good views to the north of Addingham and beyond along cliffs in 0747 (1). The hotel in 1247 can be used for lunch, snacks and toilets and accommodation (2). There is a picnic site and car park (118472) (1). The shops in Ilkley could be used to buy food/water/supplies (1). This route joins up with other trails so can explore whole area (Dales Way) (1).

DISADVANTAGES: Most of the route is over sloping land so not suitable for young families walking (1). The footpath crosses the A65 at 064498 which could be dangerous and noisy for walkers (2). There are no public telephones along the route and it is quite remote in places, so if they get into difficulties it may be hard to get help (2). There is a lack of toilet facilities (1) and there are few places to stop and buy food/water/supplies especially on the first section of the route (1). There is a steep climb in 0747 which could be dangerous, especially in winter if walkers are not careful (1).

Or any other relevant point. **4ES**

HINT Imagine you were walking this route yourself – think about what you would need.

(*f*) CBD

Main roads all lead to this square (1), there is a tourist information centre (1), and a bus station (1). There are several churches (1), and a train station (1).

Or any other relevant point. **4ES**

HINT For this question you **must** name actual buildings or features from the map.

2. An answer with well-labelled diagrams can obtain full marks.

Answers may include:

OUTWASH PLAIN: this occurs beyond the terminal moraine (1). Formed by streams created from the melting ice/glacier (1) which carry sands and small stones over a wide area (1) before sorting and depositing them in layers (1).

DRUMLIN: These are small hills made of clay (1). The clay is formed beneath the ice as rocks and other debris are ground up and smashed by the erosive power of the ice (1). After the ice melts it leaves a series of low hills – egg-shaped hills known as drumlins (1).

TERMINAL MORAINE: is formed from loose material which was carried by glacier (1) and dumped/deposited when the ice melted (1). Material is left at the end/snout of the glacier (1); this shows the maximum extent of the glacier (1). Material is unsorted (1).

Or any other relevant point. **3KU**

TOP EXAM TIP

Always try to draw diagram(s) to help you describe the processes and stages involved in your chosen feature's formation.

3. (*a*) No marks for choice.

1 mark for a simple point, 2 marks for an expanded point.

Accept negative points about the other locations.

Answers may include:

X – Closer to building for people to measure the weather (1) and to ensure the instruments are not vandalised (1). At Y children playing in the park might interfere with the weather instruments (1).

Y – Out in the open so all instruments will work properly (1). X is sheltered by the trees so instruments would give false readings (1) and rain could drip into the rain gauge (1). X may be shaded by the building giving false readings on the sunshine recorder (1). Y is on grass so rain gauge could be dug into the ground (1) whereas the tarmac at X makes it harder to locate/fix instruments (1). **3ES**

HINT To ensure accurate weather readings your site must not be sheltered or shaded by trees or buildings.

3. (continued)

(*b*) (i) 1 mark will be awarded for each correct description.

Answer: cold (1) wet (1) . **2KU**

HINT An air mass coming over the sea brings wet weather and because it is coming from the north pole it will be cold.

(ii) 1 mark will be awarded for each correct explanation.
Answers may include;

Warm/hot because coming from Southern Europe and North Africa (1), Sahara desert (1). Dry because travelling over land (1). Tropical Continental air mass (1). **2KU**

HINT Remember an air mass always brings the weather characteristics of the area it comes from.

4. (*a*) The marks allocated for this type of question are:
4 correct = 3 marks
3 or 2 correct = 2 marks
1 correct = 1 mark.

Climate Region	Graph Number
Equatorial Rain Forest	2
Tundra	1
Mediterranean	3
Hot Desert	4

3KU

HINT Start with the easily identifiable graphs first – the Tundra graph has temperatures below zero °C and the rainforest has rain and high temperatures all year round. You will then only be left with Hot Deserts and Mediterranean to figure out!

(*b*) Marks for this question can be awarded as follows: 1:3, 2:2 or 3:1.

1 mark for a simple point, 2 marks for an expanded point:

Answers may include;

ADVANTAGES: The hot, dry summer weather is ideal for a beach holiday (1) which attracts many tourists and therefore money into the area (1) and provides jobs for the locals (1). There is plenty of sunshine to ripen crops (1). The mild winters mean that crops can grow all year round (1).

DISADVANTAGES: There is a summer drought so expensive irrigation is needed for crops (1). Drought can cause water shortages (1) and restrictions on use (1). There may be a problem with forest fires during the hot dry summers (1). The local services and infrastructure might not be able to cope with the influx of tourists during the summer months (1).

Or any other relevant point. **4ES**

HINT Be careful, this question asks you what is good and bad about the climate for the locals, so make sure you answer from their viewpoint.

5. (*a*) There are 3 possible marks which will be awarded as follows:

Drawing two lines accurately to divide the graph for the missing three continents (2).

Shading each of the three sections appropriately (1). **3KU**

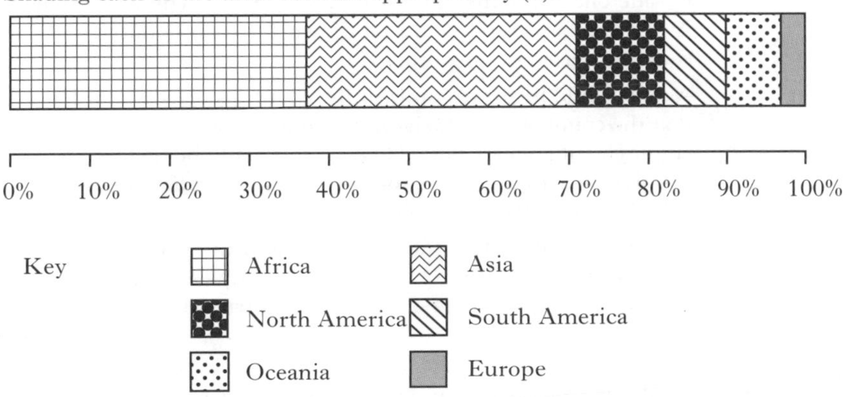

HINT Remember your divided bar graph should add up to 100% so be careful when placing your lines for the missing continents!

5. **(continued)**

(*b*) 1 mark for a simple point, 2 marks for an expanded point.

Answers may include:

Limiting the movement of animals/livestock helps to prevent overgrazing (1) as it stops all the vegetation cover being removed (1).

Irrigation provides water (1) and allows crops to be grown in the dry season (1). Wetter soils are heavier and less likely to be blown away (1).

Planting trees provides shelter which helps prevent wind erosion (1) as roots hold soil together (1). Trees also provide shade for the ground from the intense sun (1).

Stone walls built along the contours of slopes can help to trap water (1) which prevents the soil being washed away (1) so more crops can be grown in the remaining deep soil which in turn binds the soil together (1).

Advice given to farmers can help them cope with climatic change (1) and use farming techniques that will not further damage their land and increase desertification (1).

Or any other relevant point. **4KU**

HINT You must **explain** fully how your chosen method will slow down the spread of deserts – it is not enough to say "this will prevent soil erosion".

6. No marks for choice.

1 mark for a simple point, 2 marks for an expanded point.

Answers may include:

YES: Farm has a market for its produce in the town 15 km away (1). There is a mixture of high and low ground (1). The steeper land can be used for sheep farming (1) as sheep can be grazed and survive on steep slopes with poor, thin soils while crops cannot (2). The flatter ground has more fertile soil to grow crops on (1) and machinery can be used (1). There is adequate rain and warm enough temperatures to grow crops in summer (1). During the winter when temperatures are lower, the farmer can concentrate on sheep farming (1).

NO: The fairly steep slopes make it difficult to use machinery (1). The poor, thin, stony soils give only rough grazing land (1) so the farm could only support sheep farming (1). The slopes are not too steep so crops could be grown over whole farm (1). The fields are large enough for farm machinery for crop growing (1).

Or any other relevant point. **4ES**

TOP EXAM TIP

Remember that in a Yes/No type question you can give negative points about the other option.

7. At least **TWO** processing techniques must be given for full marks. Marks can be awarded as follows: 1:3, 3:1 or 2:2. Answers may include:

PROCESSING TECHNIQUES:	**REASON(S):**
Bar graph (1)	Different bar heights makes comparison between the countries very simple (1). Using colours or shading can enhance the differences (1).
Pie charts (1)	The numbers are already in percentages (1). Drawing a pie chart for each country will allow easy comparisons to be made (1) and colour could be used to highlight the different segments (1).
Divided bar graphs (1)	The figures are already in percentages so no need to spend time converting them (1). Placing the countries' divided bar graphs side by side/one above the other will make it easy to compare them (1). A divided bar graph could be drawn for each country and they could be placed in rank order (1).
Tabulating (1):	A table could be drawn up with the countries placed in order, so that the country with the largest amount of service sector employment appears first (1). The table could be further subdivided into categories to show groups of countries over 70%, between 50–70% etc (1).
Shading of world map (1):	% could be calculated into categories and the world map shaded accordingly using a key (1). This would provide a very clear visual comparison between the countries (1).

Or any other relevant point. **4ES**

HINT You must state how the actual information shown in the map could be presented in a different way, i.e. good for showing comparison **between the countries**.

8. 1 mark for a simple point, 2 marks for an expanded point.

Answers may include:

A population census is very expensive to carry out so Haiti may be unable to afford it (1). The USA can afford to carry out the census, employing many people to carry it out unlike Haiti (1). Haiti's mountainous landscape may make it more difficult to reach all villages and count everyone (1). In the USA 82% of its population live in cities so it is easier and quicker to deliver census forms to these households (1). Many people in Haiti are likely to be illiterate as they do not attend school, so cannot fill in forms (2). Lack of clean water in Haiti means disease is common therefore the population total is constantly changing and it is difficult to record and keep accurate (1).

Or any other relevant point. **4ES**

TOP EXAM TIP

This question allows you to comment on either the U.S.A.'s ease or Haiti's difficulty in carrying out a census or a mixture of both.

9. (*a*) 1 mark for each correct description from the graph.

The price of coffee has fluctuated over the years (1). Its value fell from 1980–1999 (1) from 510 cents to 200 cents in 1990 (1). Between 1991 and 2004 the price fluctuated from 200 cents to 50 cents (1). From 1996–2004 the value decreased significantly (1). After 2004 its value increased significantly (1) to 450 cents in 2009 (1). **3ES**

HINT When asked to **describe** a line graph you must give figures and dates.

(*b*) 1 mark for a simple point, 2 marks for an expanded point.

Answers may include:

YES: Uganda is very dependent on one export (1). Coffee is ¾ of everything it sells (1). If the harvest failed Uganda would not be making enough money to buy what it needed (1). Uganda is mainly buying manufactured goods (1) which are expensive and so the country may end up in debt (1). The coffee workers and plantation owners would make less money and so have less to spend, affecting other businesses in Uganda (2).

NO: Uganda still has other exports (1) and the world price/value of them may increase (1). Fair trade ensures a good price for coffee (1).

Or any other relevant point. **4ES**

HINT You can include both yes AND no arguments in your answer because you are asked your opinion, i.e. do you agree that Uganda's reliance on one main export causes it problems or not?

10. 1 mark for a simple point, 2 marks for an expanded point.

Answers may include:

Intermediate schemes tend to be low cost (1). Intermediate technology is sustainable technology (1). This means it can be repaired and kept going in poor, rural areas without great cost (1). The schemes do not require highly trained workers and so are suitable for villages in developing countries (1). The schemes are based on local resources, materials and labour so costs are kept low (1). The schemes do not require large amounts of foreign aid in the form of money or expertise (1) and as a result are likely to be less affected by tied aid arrangements (1).

For example, the fuel efficient stove made by local people using local materials would help to protect the local environment/deforestation and reduce the time spent by women collecting firewood (2).

For example, the bicycle ambulance takes a widely available product, the bike, and adapts it using basic technology into something simple and appropriate that can save lives in remote communities (2).

For example, the scheme to harvest/collect the rainwater is ideal for a developing country which is struggling with unreliable rainfall and/or drought. It uses low-cost technology tanks to collect and store rain channelled by gutters and pipes as it runs off the roofs of individual houses thus providing each family with the water it needs (2).

Or any other relevant point. **4KU**

HINT Remember – intermediate technology is suited to developing countries as it does not rely on expensive technology or expertise brought in from outside the local area.

PRACTICE EXAM B — CREDIT LEVEL WORKED ANSWERS

1. (*a*) 1 mark will be awarded for a simple point, 2 marks will be given for an expanded point.

Both river and valley must be referred to for full marks.

A maximum of 1 mark will be awarded for correct grid references.

Answers may include:

The River Einich flows in a northerly direction (1) and has a winding course (1) with several meanders (1), e.g. 922017(1); the river is joined by several tributaries, e.g. at 917003 (1). Gradient is gentle (1).

The valley floor is wide (1) up to 0.5 km wide in grid square 9100 (1) and flat (1). The sides of the valley are steep (1) and rise from about 500 metres on the valley floor to over 1000 metres, e.g. in 9000 (1). There are lakes on valley floor (9100) (1) and a very small island (919012) (1). **4KU**

HINT Make sure you only give the physical features of the river and not any human/man-made features.

(*b*) An answer with well-labelled diagrams can obtain full marks.

Answers may include:

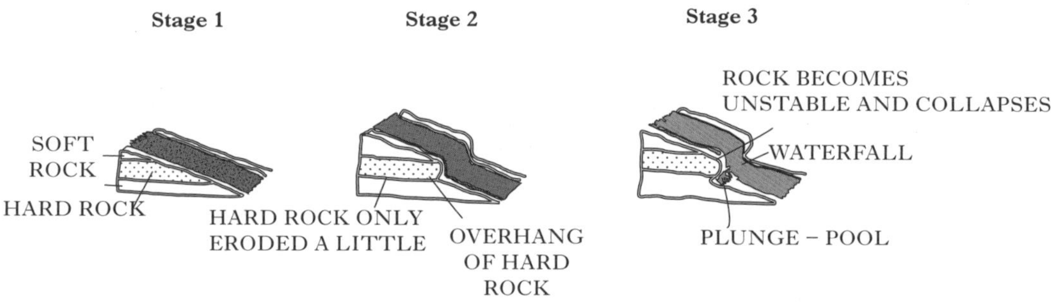

Soft rock overlain by harder rock (1). Softer or less resistant rock is worn away/eroded faster than hard rock (1), harder rock is undercut (1), the unsupported rock collapses (1), a plunge pool is formed at the bottom of the waterfall by the force of the waterfall (1) by hydraulic action (1).

Or any other relevant point. **3KU**

TOP EXAM TIP

Best answers will outline a sequence of events in a well-structured order using labelled diagrams.

(*c*) 1 mark for a simple point.

Answers must include explanation.

Answers may include:

A secondary road runs directly through the area (B970) (1) which allows heavy logging machinery and workers access to the plantations (1). It leads to Aviemore and a primary route which allows the felled trees to be transported to market (1). There is a workforce available in Aviemore or Dalfaber (1). The trees are planted on sloping land so soil is well drained (1). The height of the land means it is too cold for farming but trees can grow in the cooler temperatures (1). Trees can survive on the moderate slopes where the soil is likely to be poorer and where little else can grow (1). The slopes are not suitable for arable farming as they restrict the use of machinery (1). Land is beside river so risk of flooding makes it unsuitable for building or arable farming, i.e. land is not suitable for any other land use (1).

Accept any other relevant point. **4KU**

HINT Remember that commercial forestry is growing trees for money so treat this like an industrial location question with forestry being the business.

(*d*) 1 mark will be awarded for a simple point; you will get 2 marks for an expanded point.

Negative points against alternatives are acceptable.

A maximum of 1 mark will be awarded for correct grid references.

1. (continued)

Answers may include:

SERVICE CENTRE: it has numerous services for residents (1): 2 churches (1), a railway station (1) at 896124 (1). All roads in the area lead to Aviemore (1). A school for local children (1) is located at 894134 (1). There is also a post office (1) at 897127 (1).

TOURISM & RECREATION: Tourist information centre (1) is located at 895119 (1). The attraction of Aviemore and its surrounding area includes its beautiful mountain scenery (1) with footpaths leading out of town into the surrounding hills and forest areas (1), e.g. in 8812 (1) and viewpoint in 888122 (1). The Aviemore Centre (1) at 893125(1). Camping and caravan site (1) at 893117 (1). Parking is available at 893125 (1). National Cycle Network through 8912 (1).

Or any other relevant point. **5ES**

HINT If an area is good for tourism there will be many blue tourist symbols found there. For a service centre, look to see what facilities and buildings exist there for the local residents to use.

(*e*) 1 mark will be awarded for a simple point; you will get 2 marks for an expanded point.

Note that no marks are awarded in this question for correct grid references.

Answers may include:

YES: It will be a good place to generate wind power because it is high and exposed, therefore likely to be windy, on top of the hill (1). The wind turbines will not create air pollution (1). There are very few houses for miles around so there will be few protests from local residents (1). The turbines could be placed below the summit so there would be less visual pollution (1). There are no trees that would need to be cut down for the turbines or to create access (1).

NO: Local people might complain that the turbines are an eyesore (1). There might be some noise pollution for the surrounding area (1). Animals and especially birds might be disturbed by the turbines (1). The wind turbines on Castle Hill might affect tourist numbers to one of Scotland's most scenic and popular tourist areas (1). The steep mountain slopes would make it difficult to use heavy machinery (1). There is no road to transport machinery and workers to the site during construction (1). It is far away from any big settlements so it would be expensive to transmit electricity from Castle Hill (1). Wind turbines on Castle Hill would spoil the view from the footpath for walkers (1) and the building of the wind farm and the noise of the turbines would cause conflict with hill walkers (1). The turbines may conflict with the aims of a national park (1).

Or any other relevant point. **6ES**

HINT When thinking about any new proposal/development, try to imagine who would benefit from the new project and who might object to it, i.e. the local people? wildlife? the scenery?

(*f*) At least 2 techniques must be given for full marks.

Marks for this question can be awarded as follows: 2:3 or 3:2.

You will be awarded a maximum of 3 marks if no reasons are given or if you only refer to one technique.

Answers may include:

Visit the footpath and take measurements (1): By measuring the width of the footpath the pupils could see for themselves evidence of erosion at different points (1). This information could be drawn on an annotated field sketch so that certain areas could be highlighted (1). If measurements were taken at a later date in the same places on the footpath then it would be possible to gather further evidence of any erosion (1).

Observe and record the number of walkers/sightseers using the footpath (1); this will give an indication as to how busy the area is (1) and you could see if people were straying from the designated footpaths or dropping litter (1).

Take photographs at different points along the footpath (1). This will allow comparisons to be made along the route (1) to see if some points are being more heavily eroded as it would show the bare/damaged ground (1). These could also be compared with other photographs taken at other times to see if there have been any changes along the path (1).

Field sketch of the footpath (1). Pupils could select what information they gathered (1) and what they thought relevant and important enough to include on the sketch (1).

1. **(continued)**

Interview walkers (1). Walkers would be able to give an opinion about the visual damage/drainage problems along the path (1) and this provides up-to-date first-hand information (1).

Or any other relevant point. **5ES**

HINT For full marks you must give reasons and remember to relate each technique to the actual question asked, e.g. "interview walkers".

2. A maximum of 1 mark will be given for simple descriptions or a list of weather characteristics.

A maximum of 2 marks will be awarded if you give a correct description of the weather.

Remember, your answers must include explanations.

Answers may include:

High pressure/anticyclone is currently covering Scotland (1). Skies will be clear due to the lack of any fronts (1). Winter anticyclones (January) bring cold overnight temperatures, often below freezing (1), which result in ground frost and icy roads (1).

Anticyclones usually have light winds as indicated by the widely spaced isobars (1). Light winds blow clockwise around anticyclones which give a westerly (W) wind in Scotland (1).

A warm front will move over Scotland later in the day (1) increasing cloud cover (1) and, due to the cold air temperatures, snow is likely to fall (1). There is the possibility of blizzard conditions (1) due to tightening isobars (1) making driving conditions very difficult.

Or any other relevant point. **5KU**

TOP EXAM TIP

Always read the title on top of the synoptic chart to find out what time of year the chart is showing.

3. Agree/disagree answers are acceptable.

Note that no marks will be given for straight copies from the reference diagram.

Answers may include:

AGREE: Jobs have been created in the area reducing unemployment (1) and bringing income into Alaska (1). Pipeline is mainly in very remote and isolated parts of the country so causes little visual pollution to locals (1). Very few people will be affected by the oil drilling operations because few live here (1). The oil provides cheaper energy for locals' homes and factories (1). The pipe is raised high off the ground in places to allow wildlife like caribou to pass under the pipe (1). The construction of the pipeline would have attracted tens of thousands of workers to Alaska and caused a massive economic boom in towns up and down the 800 mile pipeline route (1). With the world's oil resources depleting, the oil will be even more valuable in future and bring more money into the area (1). The tourists attracted to the pipeline bring money and jobs to the area (1) as they require hotels, restaurants, tour guides etc (1).

DISAGREE: The 800 mile long pipeline flows through an unspoiled natural environment and ruins the landscape (1). The pipeline runs beside Arctic National Wildlife Refuge Reserve so might affect the wildlife there (1). The pipeline may upset animal trails such as the migrating caribou herds (1) and carries with it the potential of a devastating leak or spill that would destroy fragile habitats and animals (1). Possible leaking of oil into Copper River tributaries would damage a world-famous salmon fishery and pollute the river (1). The valuable oil is mostly exported, so the rest of America and the world benefit from the resource, not the Alaskan people (1). Possible earthquakes on faults along the pipeline route present a potential threat (1).

Or any other relevant point. **6ES**

HINT Use information from both the map and the diagram to answer this but remember not to simply copy out the question! You must explain why you think the pipeline has either helped or spoiled life for the locals and the area.

4. 1 mark will be awarded for a simple point; you will get 2 marks for an expanded point.

Answers may include:

A corner shop is a low order service so will have a small sphere of influence (1). Low order services are used frequently by people and are numerous in number so people are not prepared to travel long distances for convenience goods like bread and milk (2).

A shoe shop is a middle order service so will have a larger sphere of influence than a corner shop (1). People are willing to travel a long distance to get to a high order service like a large department store so therefore this has a very large sphere of influence (1).

4. **(continued)**

A department store sells more expensive goods and has a much greater choice, i.e. it sells more specialist products that you might shop around for before going ahead and buying something, so therefore people are willing to travel to get there (2).

Or any other relevant point. **4ES**

HINT: The sphere of influence of a service is how far people will travel to make use of that service.

5. 1 mark will be awarded for a simple point; you will get 2 marks for an expanded point.

A maximum of 1 mark will be given for a basic description, e.g. 'beside a main road, close to university' etc. without an explanation of why this is good for an industry.

Answers may include:

Good transport links

Good road infrastructure is needed to bring raw materials to the factory and to deliver finished products to the market (1) and to allow workers easy access to and from their work (1). A nearby railway station allows staff to commute easily to work (1). Being close to an international airport allows managers and overseas buyers access to the industry (1) and enables worldwide transportation of small, high-value, lightweight products (1). Access to a port would facilitate worldwide distribution of goods to overseas markets (1).

Pleasant environment

A pleasant environment will mean that the industry can attract the best, most highly-skilled staff as they are willing to work and live in such an area (1). A high quality environment is also important as workers' attitudes, productivity and work rate will all be improved in better surroundings (1). Leisure facilities such as golf courses may also be important for owners and managers when considering suitable industrial location (1).

Suitable factory site

Industry requires an area of flat land on which to build its large factory (1) with space for large car parks and possible expansion (1). Sites on the edge of the city may be more attractive to modern industry as land is cheaper (1) and it is away from the congestion of the CBD so less time is wasted in traffic (1).

Proximity to universities and colleges

Industries can use the nearby university/college to help with their research and development (1). Near to skilled and educated graduates that they can employ as workers (1). Industries can make use of the research and new ideas from the universities/colleges to enhance their products and designs (1).

Neighbouring industries

If there is a concentration of similar industries in an area then the industries can supply materials/ components to each other (1) at reduced transport costs (1). Similar industries may also be able to share ideas or save on research costs if they work together (1).

Government assistance

Government incentives may make an area more attractive to a company as they may help with the huge start-up costs involved in setting up a business (1), e.g. by giving grants, subsidies, loans or help with staff training costs in an area of high unemployment (2).

Or any other relevant point. **6KU**

HINT: Use the picture in Reference Diagram Q5A to remind you of the type of light, modern industry you are to consider locating and answer appropriately.

6. (*a*) 1 mark will be awarded for a simple point; you will get 2 marks for an expanded point. Answers may include:

Farm X produces more crops than Y as the land is flatter and more fertile (1). Arable farming requires a lot more part-time workers especially at harvest time (1). Farm X is warmer and drier than Y so more suited to crop growing (1). Farm X is nearer to the market/town to sell its crops while fresh, e.g. strawberries (1). The proximity to the town also helps to lower transport costs (1).

Farm Y's steeper slopes mean the machinery is less effective (1). Sheep are hardy animals and only they can survive in the cold, damp weather (1). Poor thin, stony soils are unsuitable for growing crops (1). Some turnips are grown as fodder crops for the sheep in winter (1). Fewer workers are needed to tend sheep than for an arable farm where jobs such as spraying fertiliser, weeding etc. are more labour intensive (1).

Or any other relevant point. **5ES**

> *HINT* HINT – This question, 6(a), is really asking you first to identify the likely farm type of X and Y and then explain your choice from the information provided.

(*b*) You should give at least 2 processing techniques in order to get full marks for this question.

Marks for this question can be awarded as follows: 2:3 or 3:2.

You will be awarded a maximum of 3 marks if no reasons are given or if you only refer to one technique.

Answers may include:

PROCESSING TECHNIQUES:	**REASON(S):**
Bar graphs (1) or a multiple bar graph (1)	Drawing 2 bar graphs (one for each farm) or a multiple bar graph to show the different machinery will allow easy comparisons to be made (1). Different colours can be used to show the differences between the two farms (1).
Pie charts to show farm output (1)	The two farms' output data is already in percentages (1). Drawing 2 pie charts – 1 for each farm – will allow easy comparisons to be made (1). Colour can be used to highlight the different segments (1).
Divided bar graphs (1)	A series of individual divided bar graphs for each farm would show the different proportion of farm output for each farm (1); the sections could be drawn in rank order to highlight the largest and smallest outputs on each farm(1).
Pictograms (1)	A series of pictures of output or machinery for both farms could be drawn giving a clear visual comparison between the two farms (1). The illustrations may be easier to interpret without having to look at a key (like you would have to do for the pie charts and divided bar graphs (1).

Or any other relevant point. **5ES**

> *HINT* You must give **different** reasons for each technique, e.g. you can't write "differences will be enhanced with colour" for pie charts and bar graphs and expect 2 marks!

7. (*a*) One mark will be awarded for each valid point.

Remember, your answer should be a description.

Answers may include:

Tanzania has much wider base than Italy (1).

Over 6% of Tanzania's population is under 5 years old compared with only 4% of Italy's (1). Tanzania's population drops rapidly after age 30 whereas Italy's begins to increase (1).

Italy has a much larger working age population (1).

Many more people survive into old age (over 65) in Italy (1) with around 2% over 85 years old (1).

3ES

> *HINT* For this question you should compare the % of children under 15, those of working age and the elderly populations of both countries.

(*b*) 1 mark will be awarded for a simple point; you will get 2 marks for an expanded point. Answers may include:

Italy is a developed country whereas Tanzania is a developing country (1).

In Tanzania birth rates are high because there is little access to family planning (1) whereas in Italy this is widely available (1).

In Tanzania birth rates are high because young people are needed to support old age/illness (1) whereas in Italy health care and pensions provision make this unnecessary (1).

In Tanzania birth rates are high because young people can earn wages from working, adding to family incomes (1) and because young people can help out on the family farm (1) whereas in Italy education is compulsory to 16 years of age (1).

7. (continued)

In Tanzania birth rates are high because females have little access to higher education/careers (1). In Italy many females want careers and so put off having children while this is pursued (1).

Or any other relevant point. **5KU**

HINT Make sure you **explain** each difference you have identified in part 'a' fully and do not just repeat yourself by writing opposites, e.g. good healthcare in Italy v bad healthcare in Tanzania.

8. 1 mark will be awarded for a simple point; you will get 2 marks for an expanded point.

Answers may include:

Malawi's main export is foodstuffs (88%) (1) which are raw materials which sell for a low price (1).

It mainly buys manufactured goods and fuels (1); these are processed, expensive products which demand a high price (1). The country makes a trade deficit/loss of £112 million a year (1).

Malawi mainly sells to the E.U. and USA, i.e. developed countries (1). It mainly buys from other African nations (1). The country it imports the most from is South Africa (1).

Or any other relevant point. **5ES**

HINT A country's trade balance is the difference between the value of its imports and exports. In Malawi's case they spend more on imports than they make from exports so it is making a trade deficit or loss.

9. 1 mark will be awarded for a simple point; you will get 2 marks for an expanded point.

Answers may include:

Headquarters are usually located in a developed country because:

Money/wealth tends to be concentrated in developed world countries (1). Industry has been established in these countries for a long time (1). Developed countries have the most economic power and have strong trade links (1). Countries like the USA have the highly educated people required to manage large companies (1). Companies like Nike often want to keep their decision making headquarters in the part of the world they started up (1). Developed countries have the transport infrastructure and communication networks required by large multinational headquarters (1).

Branches/factories are normally located in developing nations because:

Low labour costs encourage investment (1). Often developing countries have less stringent labour laws and fewer or less powerful trade unions so workers can be forced to work longer hours with fewer breaks for little money (2). The massive potential market in developing countries with their growing populations encourages multinational corporations (MNCs) to open there (1). Often, developing countries have less strict pollution controls and this attracts companies as this often lowers costs (1). Companies may quickly move their factories to other countries if it works out cheaper for them elsewhere (1). Land and building costs for factories are considerably lower than in developed nations (1). Often governments of poorer nations offer subsidies to MNCs to try and attract them to invest in their country (1).

Or any other relevant point. **5KU**

HINT You need to explain why the headquarters are in the richer countries as well as why the factories are in poorer nations for full marks.

10. 1 mark will be awarded for a simple point; you will get 2 marks for an expanded point.

Answers may include:

YES: As much of the aid is 'tied aid', aid has to be spent in the country that gives the aid (1) so it helps companies in the donor country (1) and provides jobs (1). Giving aid also helps trade; if developing countries become richer they will buy more goods from the developed countries (1). Taking the aid means the donor country has to support the developing country in times of crises, e.g. a war (1). Reference Diagram Q10A shows that most countries think it is a good idea to give some aid (1) for example, countries like Norway and Denmark donate around 0·8% of their GDP to developing nations (1).

NO: Countries are not that keen to give aid as none of them even gives away 1% of overall GDP (1) for example, Italy and the U.S.A. give less than 0·2% of their GDP annually (1). Countries are very cautious about giving aid in case their own economy suffers, especially in times of recession (1). The money spent on aid could be invested in their own country (1).

Or any other relevant point. **4ES**